Home Office Research Study 258

Youth homelessness and substance use: report to the drugs and alcohol research unit

Dr Emma Wincup, Gemma Buckland and Rhianon Bayliss

The views expressed in this report are those of the authors, not necessarily those of the Home Office (nor do they reflect Government policy).

Home Office Research, Development and Statistics Directorate
February 2003

Home Office Research Studies

The Home Office Research Studies are reports on research undertaken by or on behalf of the Home Office. They cover the range of subjects for which the Home Secretary has responsibility. Other publications produced by the Research, Development and Statistics Directorate include Findings, Statistical Bulletins and Statistical Papers.

The Research, Development and Statistics Directorate

RDS is part of the Home Office. The Home Office's purpose is to build a safe, just and tolerant society in which the rights and responsibilities of individuals, families and communities are properly balanced and the protection and security of the public are maintained.

RDS is also part of National Statistics (NS). One of the aims of NS is to inform Parliament and the citizen about the state of the nation and provide a window on the work and performance of government, allowing the impact of government policies and actions to be assessed.

Therefore –

Research Development and Statistics Directorate exists to improve policy making, decision taking and practice in support of the Home Office purpose and aims, to provide the public and Parliament with information necessary for informed debate and to publish information for future use.

First published 2003

Application for reproduction should be made to the Communication Development Unit, Room 201, Home Office, 50 Queen Anne's Gate, London SW1H 9AT.

© Crown copyright 2003   ISBN   1 84082 965 6

ISSN   0072 6435

Foreword

This report is one of five research reports published as part of the Vulnerable Groups Research Programme. The central focus of the programme was to investigate patterns of drug use among groups of vulnerable young people and their access to services. Each project focuses on a different group of vulnerable young people, who tend not to be included in the general population surveys. The project reported on here concentrates on homeless young people. The four others examine: young people involved in sex work, care leavers and runaways, young drug users who are in contact with drugs services and young people in contact with youth offending teams. Many of the young people across these projects are likely to have had similar backgrounds and vulnerabilities. A number of the studies explore this area and the degree to which the young people are in fact the same population caught at different points in their lives and via different services.

The main aim of this study is to provide a detailed account of homeless young people's substance use to inform future prevention and treatment work with this group. The consensus from a small number of previous research studies suggests that levels of substance use amongst homeless young people are considerably higher than that of the general population. A number of recent policy documents also identify homeless young people as a particularly vulnerable group and suggest that drug misuse contributes to and exacerbates their homeless situation. Such findings highlight the importance of strong links between drugs services and homelessness agencies.

Tom Bucke
Programme Director, Drugs and Alcohol Research,
Research, Development and Statistics Directorate

Acknowledgements

The authors would like to thank all of the projects providing services for young homeless people that were involved in the study, in particular the young people and staff that agreed to be interviewed. We are also grateful to Jane Fountain, and colleagues at the University of Kent, in particular Neil Hunt who provided useful comments on the draft interview schedule.

Emma Wincup
Gemma Buckland
Kent Criminal Justice Centre, University of Kent at Canterbury

Rhianon Bayliss
School of Social Sciences, Cardiff University

Researchers working on the Drugs and Alcohol Research Programme would like to thank Jane Fountain of the University of Central Lancashire and Mike Shiner of the London School of Economics for acting as independent assessors for this report.

Contents

List of tables

List of figures

Summary

This report presents the findings of a research study of substance[1] use amongst homeless young people (25 and under) in England and Wales. It is one of the five research studies that form the Home Office Drug Research Programme on patterns of drug use among vulnerable groups of young people. Youth homelessness and substance use are both major social problems in England and Wales today, complicated by their strong relationships with other aspects of social exclusion. Both areas have been subject to a number of policy interventions in recent years, and attempts have been made to improve the evidence-base to guide future activity. However, substance use amongst homeless young people has received little focused attention by researchers. The limited research available suggests that levels of substance use amongst this group are much higher than those of 'housed' young people.

Research design

The overall aim of the research was to provide a detailed account of substance use amongst homeless young people that could be used to inform future prevention and treatment activity.

1. To map out patterns of substance use amongst homeless young people.
2. To analyse their involvement in risky behaviours which impact on health.
3. To explore the backgrounds of homeless young people and in particular to highlight risk factors which make them vulnerable to problem substance use.
4. To examine homeless young people's access to drugs information, drugs services and health services, to consider actual and potential barriers and suggest ways of overcoming them.

The research involved a range of research methods leading to the collection of qualitative and quantitative data. Over an 18 month period beginning in January 2001, data were gathered in four case study areas in England and Wales: Birmingham, Brighton and Hove, Canterbury and Cardiff. The main methods were interviews with 160 young people aged 25 and under, recruited through homelessness agencies in the four case study areas, and 22 interviews with professionals who work with homeless young people.

---

1. This includes drugs, alcohol, tobacco and the illicit use of prescribed medication, over the counter medicines and volatile substances.

Key findings

The main findings of the study can be summarised as follows:

Substance use

Homeless young people reported high lifetime, last year and last month prevalence rates for drug use (illegal drugs and illicit use of prescribed medication). Ninety-five per cent of them had used drugs. Often they had begun experimenting with illegal drugs at a young age, typically aged 14. Levels of use of cannabis, amphetamine and ecstasy were particularly high, but a substantial minority had used heroin and crack cocaine. Current patterns of drug use were diverse. Seventeen per cent of the sample was identified as problem drug users and a further 14 per cent had been problem drug users in the past. Whilst many drug users took measures to ensure that their drug taking was as safe as possible, the data gathered suggests evidence of some risky behaviours. These include poly-drug use and unsafe injecting practices. Almost one-quarter (23%) had accidentally overdosed on drugs or alcohol.

Almost all the young people interviewed smoked on a daily basis. It was evident that many young people were increasing the health risks of smoking by smoking hand-rolled cigarettes without filters and mixing tobacco with illegal drugs. Current patterns of alcohol use were diverse. Whilst 18 per cent of the sample did not drink at all, a considerable proportion was adopting risky drinking patterns: frequently exceeding sensible daily limits and binge drinking. Fourteen per cent of the sample was identified as problem drinkers.

Homelessness

The young people interviewed frequently became homeless for the first time at an early age, and for over half the sample this followed episodes of running away. Substance use was the second most common explanation for homelessness but this was not always problem substance use, and sometimes was only one of a number of reasons given. Other common reasons for becoming homeless were family conflict and experiences of abuse. Experiences of rough sleeping at some point in their lives amongst the sample were high. This reflects the finding that they sometimes became homeless with little warning and were not aware of where they could go to get help. Young people faced multiple barriers when attempting to access temporary and permanent accommodation. Substance use was cited by the young people as one of many barriers they faced, and service providers echoed this view.

Consequences of homelessness and substance use

The relationship between substance use and homelessness is complex, and the young people's accounts suggest that whilst becoming homeless can lead to an escalation of substance use it can also provide an opportunity to give up or cut down.

One-fifth of interviewees who reported health problems attributed them solely to substance use. Homelessness, particularly sleeping rough, appeared to have a detrimental effect on the physical health of almost half the young people interviewed. Poor access to health care was rarely mentioned as a problem. Instead young people felt other aspects of homelessness had a greater impact such as poor diets and lack of shelter and warmth. Levels of mental health problems were disproportionately high amongst young homeless people. Seventy per cent had been diagnosed with depression or other mental health problem, or had concerns about their mental health.

Substance use and homelessness had consequent implications for offending. Ninety-five per cent of young people had committed an offence at some point in their lives. A quarter of young people linked offences with alcohol use and half with drug use; one-third related offences to homelessness. Experiences of victimisation were also common amongst the sample.

Access to services

The strongest message emerging from the research regarding service access was the need for dedicated and appropriate provision for young people, which addresses their substance use within the context of the many other problems that they experience. This applies equally to homelessness and substance misuse services.

Prevention of substance use

Prevention activities with young homeless people were limited but there is considerable scope for prevention work with this group. However, there are a number of barriers to successful prevention work, particularly the possibility of resistance from some young people, legal constraints and the lack of expertise in many homelessness services.

Recommendations

In tackling problem substance use and homelessness, the key players are substance misuse services; drug action teams; homelessness agencies; local authorities and other providers of social housing and health services. The importance of partnerships between agencies in order to be able to respond appropriately and adequately to the needs of young homeless people cannot be overemphasised. Partnership should be central to all service planning, design and delivery. It is important that each key player individually and collectively develops strategies to tackle homelessness, problem substance use and related issues.

Tackling substance use

- A number of harm reduction activities could be usefully targeted at homeless young people. These include: highlighting the possible dangers of poly-drug use; raising awareness of the health risks of drug use, particularly injecting; reminding intravenous drug users of safer injecting practices and the importance of avoiding injecting in the presence of others because of the risk that it might lead to others injecting; promoting awareness of ways of avoiding accidental overdoses; and providing drug users with the necessary skills to cope with incidents of overdose by their peers.

- Given the findings of this study it would appear that prevention activity aimed at this group needs to emphasise the dangers of binge drinking and to encourage drinking within sensible daily limits.

- Whilst it would be preferable to support young people in their attempts to give up smoking, inevitably some will continue to smoke. Hence harm reduction activity could be geared towards highlighting the dangers of smoking cigarettes without filters.

- Attention should be given to how drugs agencies, GP surgeries and homelessness agencies might provide appropriate information for young people. Training in substance use issues should be provided for more staff in homelessness services.

- Treatment services that address substance use should recognise the complexity of other issues experienced by homeless young people. This may be achieved by the provision of discrete, dedicated services for young people, by appointing dedicated young peoples' workers in substance misuse agencies, or by expanding drop-in services. Services could be brought to homeless young people at homelessness service premises by means of regular services and surgeries run by primary care, drugs and alcohol services' workers, or through outreach work at young peoples' centres. More innovative work could be developed with young substance users, for example, mentoring or diversion activities such as music or sport, which aim to encourage young people to develop interests other than substance use.

Tackling homelessness

The research findings suggest the need for the following actions to be developed further:

- prevention activities targeting in particular those young people at risk of becoming homeless;
- early interventions to enable young people to retain their current accommodation (the provision of drop-in advice centres for young people (or 'one stop shops') where they can access advice on a range of issues is one possible model);
- development of services for young people who run away before they are 16;
- prioritisation of support for young rough sleepers;
- provision of dedicated services for young people aged between 16 and 25;
- the need to promote awareness of services that are available for homeless young people; and
- floating support packages to enable them to sustain tenancies in social or private housing, and supported housing for some groups of young people.

The difficulties young people faced in finding housing were exacerbated by current benefit policies, particularly the single room rent, which is in need of review.

Promoting health

- Difficulties remain in accessing mental health services and this needs urgent attention.
- Education and training amongst general health professionals and their staff are necessary to eliminate stereotypical and negative attitudes and beliefs about homeless young people, where these still exist.
- Promoting health amongst homeless young people is not simply about promoting access to health care. It requires tackling the other health inequalities they experience. For example, providing vitamins and vaccinations, and creating healthier environments in hostels and night shelters.

This report presents the findings of a study on substance use amongst young homeless people in England and Wales. It is one of a number of research studies within the Home Office Drug Research Programme on vulnerable groups and drug use. The study will be introduced by a brief description of relevant academic literature and the policy background to current practice and a discussion of the research design.

Some working definitions

Youth homelessness

There are no fixed definitions of homelessness but it is useful to think of homelessness as a continuum, ranging from 'rooflessness' or sleeping rough, to living in bed and breakfast accommodation and hostels, to an inability to leave unsatisfactory housing conditions (Rugg, 2000). Distinctions are often made in academic research between the 'visible homeless' such as rough sleepers and hostel and night shelter residents, and the 'hidden homeless' such as those staying temporarily with family and friends. The term 'homeless' is used throughout this report mainly to describe rough sleepers or others who are insecurely housed and accessing services such as hostels, day centres and night shelters. However, the term is also used to refer to young people who are living in supported housing or their own accommodation with floating support[2]. All those involved in this research were continuing to access homelessness services. Without support these young people were at risk of losing their tenancies.

What constitutes homelessness may be contested but it is clear that homeless people are a heterogeneous group with diverse social, economic and health needs, hence the trend within the research literature to perceive homelessness as more than a housing problem (Fitzpatrick and Klinker, 2000). For example common problems experienced by homeless people of all ages include health problems, unemployment and poverty.

In the UK the term 'youth homelessness' generally refers to homelessness amongst young single people aged between 16 and 25 (Hutson and Liddiard, 1994). This definition of 'youth' was largely adopted for the purposes of this study, however, interviews were also conducted with a small number of young women who were either pregnant or had children,

---

2.   Outreach support to help young people to sustain their tenancy and enable them to live in independent accommodation provided by local authorities and housing associations.

and young people who were seeking accommodation with a partner. Defining young people as those aged between 16 and 25 is for the most part in keeping with that adopted in UK drug policies, which suggest that young people are those aged up to 25 (President of the Council, 1998; National Assembly for Wales, 2000a).

Substance use

For the purposes of this report substance use refers to the use of alcohol, illegal drugs and tobacco, and the illicit use of prescribed medication, over-the counter remedies and volatile substances. The need for distinctions to be made is recognised but it is beneficial for research to look at all forms of substance use together, not least because individuals frequently use a combination of substances.

Commonly used terms to describe substance use include experimental, recreational, problematic and chaotic, and these are based more on individual opinion than accepted definitions (Health Advisory Service, 2001). The Advisory Council on the Misuse of Drugs (1998) defines a problem drug user as any person who experiences social, psychological, physical or legal problems related to intoxication and or regular excessive consumption and or dependence as a consequence of his/her own use of drugs or other chemical substances; and anyone whose drug misuse involves, or may lead to, the sharing of injecting equipment. DrugScope defines recreational drug use as 'the use of drugs for pleasure or leisure', with the implication that drug use has become part of someone's lifestyle, even though they may only take drugs occasionally (www.drugscope.org.uk). The research team adopted these definitions. Chapter 3 explores how these were operationalised. However, unambiguous distinctions between different patterns of substance use are difficult to draw, largely because all forms of substance use can produce problems.

Background

Risk and protective factors: recognising vulnerable groups

A growing body of research has sought to identify the risk factors associated with problem drug use, and this has included some analysis of social, as well as individual, factors. Clayton (1992) offers a useful definition of a risk factor as an individual attribute or characteristic, situational condition, or environmental context that increases the probability of drug use or abuse or a transition in the level of involvement with drugs. Conversely a protective factor inhibits, reduces, or buffers drug use. Risk factors can relate to the family (for example, parental or sibling drug use, family disruption, poor attachment to or communication with parents, and child abuse); school (for example, poor education performance, truancy and exclusion); involvement in crime and other conduct disorders such as truancy; mental disorder; social deprivation, and young age of onset (Lloyd, 1998). Lloyd suggests that one key feature of the risk literature is its interconnectedness and thus risk factors are best viewed as a 'web of causation' (Lloyd, 1998: 217). Based on research findings it is possible to identify high risk or vulnerable groups such as homeless people, and this has led to an increasing practice focus on prevention and early intervention work with such groups (see for example, Health Advisory Service, 2001).

Policy developments

Given the complexity of substance use and youth homelessness as social problems, many social policies may potentially overcome some of the difficulties experienced by homeless young people. The focus here is only on the most significant developments.

In 1998, *Tackling Drugs to Build a Better Britain* (President of the Council, 1998) was launched as the Government's ten-year strategy for tackling drug misuse, and this was followed in 2000 by *Tackling Substance Misuse in Wales* (National Assembly for Wales, 2000a). Both strategies identify the homeless as one group at particular risk of developing patterns of problem substance use; both focus on the young (i.e. those under 25) and dedicate one of their four aims to helping young people resist substance misuse to achieve their full potential in society. Action promised, which may impact on young homeless people, includes appropriate and specific prevention intervention for 'at risk' groups; improvements to the range and quality of treatment services for the under 25s and promoting access to specific support services for young people. More detailed action is outlined in the Health Advisory Service (2001) report, *The Substance of Young Needs*. This focuses on young people aged up to 19 and makes recommendations for the commissioning, design and delivery of services and interventions. Again young homeless people are identified as a vulnerable group, and it is suggested that drug misuse contributes to, and exacerbates, their homeless situation. Thus strong links need to be made between drugs services and homeless agencies.

In 1999, the Rough Sleepers Unit was established and published a national strategy for reducing the number of rough sleepers (Rough Sleepers Unit, 1999). The strategy promised a radical new approach to help vulnerable rough sleepers off the street, rebuilding the lives of former rough sleepers and preventing new rough sleepers of tomorrow. It was recognised that young people, by virtue of their age, were vulnerable and included specific proposals to help them such as providing emergency accommodation and family mediation. Those who misuse drugs and alcohol were defined as a vulnerable group and appropriate support for this group was emphasised. The strategy also recognised that rough sleepers with physical or mental health problems have traditionally had poor access to health care services (for reports on progress see Rough Sleepers Unit 2000; 2001). Work on rough sleeping is now being complemented by activity to tackle homelessness in all its forms (Homelessness Directorate, 2002). Homelessness has been similarly prioritised in Wales. A report on rough sleeping (National Assembly for Wales, 2000b) and the establishment of a homeless commission which reported in 2001 (National Assembly for Wales, 2001) has culminated in the publication of a draft homelessness strategy (National Assembly for Wales, 2002).

Previous research

A number of national government surveys provide data on patterns of substance use amongst the general population, including young people. The British Crime Survey (BCS) provides data on self-reported drug use and the General Household Survey asks a series of questions on an individual's use of alcohol. Although young people are included in these surveys, the number of young respondents is generally small, and data are collected from individuals in households. They therefore exclude homeless young people. Attempts have been made to overcome this by examining self-reported drug use among those that have previously been homeless using the Youth Lifestyles Survey (Goulden and Sondhi, 2001). However, very small numbers were identified and the fact that they were housed at the time of the interview means they are unlikely to be representative of the homeless population. Nevertheless the study found 'apparent but not substantial differences' (p.25) between those who had experienced homelessness and those who had not, with rates highest among those who had ever slept rough.

A literature review was conducted as part of the research report here and it was noted that few studies (exceptions include Flemen, 1997 and Hammersley and Pearl, 1997) have specifically examined the extent of substance use among homeless young people (see Wincup and Bayliss, 2001). There are, however, a number of related types of research studies.

1. Studies of the extent of substance use amongst homeless people of all ages (Fountain and Howes, 2002)
2. Studies of drug users' experiences of homelessness (Cox and Lawless, 1999; Neale, 2001)
3. Studies of drug users accessed through homelessness agencies (*Big Issue* in the North, 1999; Klee and Reid, 1998)
4. Broader studies of youth homelessness which have been able to comment on substance use by this group (Carlen, 1996).

All have highlighted the difficulties of understanding the complex links between substance use and homelessness, particularly as homelessness and substance use often coalesce with other facets of social exclusion. The emerging consensus from studies completed to date is that levels of substance use amongst homeless young people are considerably higher than those of 'housed' young people.

Methodology

Aims and objectives

The overall aim of the research was to provide a detailed account of substance use amongst young homeless people that could be used to inform future prevention and treatment activity.

1. To map out patterns of substance use amongst young homeless people.
2. To analyse their involvement in risky behaviours which impact on health.
3. To explore the backgrounds of young homeless people and in particular to highlight risk factors which make them vulnerable to problem substance use.
4. To examine young homeless people's access to drugs information, drugs services and health services, to consider actual and potential barriers and suggest ways of overcoming them.

The research involved a range of research methods leading to the collection of qualitative and quantitative data. Over an 18 month period from January 2001, data were gathered in four case study areas in England and Wales: Birmingham, Brighton and Hove, Canterbury and Cardiff. They are not claimed to be representative of all cities in England and Wales, but were selected to incorporate a broad cross-section in terms of size, known homelessness and drug problems. The main methods used were interviews with young homeless people and professionals who work with them.

Interviews with young people

The research team conducted interviews with 160 young people aged 25 and under who were in contact with homelessness services. These divided almost equally across the four case studies. It is difficult to define the characteristics of a population such as homeless young people who may be hidden, and thus difficult to construct a sample that would reflect the wider population of homeless young people. Consequently, the sample was not recruited in a statistically random way. Instead purposive sampling techniques were employed in order to gain access to different experiences of homelessness, for example rough sleeping, living in hostels and staying with friends on a temporary basis, and to explore the different experiences of young people of different ages, sex and ethnic origins. In each area young people were contacted through key organisations, both in the voluntary and statutory sector, that provided services for young homeless people. Efforts were made to include a variety of agencies reflecting different forms of provision available. Drugs and alcohol services were deliberately avoided as a route for accessing research participants to avoid skewing the data collected on patterns of substance use.

The young people were reached via 28 agencies[3]. These included:

- day centres for homeless people of all ages and for young people specifically;
- *Big Issue* distribution centres;
- hostels, including hostels for young women and for young people;
- a foyer providing housing for young people with low support needs to enable them to participate in employment, education and training;
- drop-in housing advice centres, including specialist centres for young people;
- housing providers e.g. housing associations and city councils (including outreach teams);
- a resettlement centre;
- a project providing activities for socially excluded young people; and
- supported shared accommodation.

Agency staff and homeless young people were asked to identify other potential interviewees to obtain access to the hidden homeless, for example young people waiting to get a place in a hostel.

The interviews investigated a wide range of issues and responses were recorded on a questionnaire[4] that included both closed and open-ended questions. The interview was divided into seven sections covering personal characteristics; experiences of homelessness; health issues (physical and mental health, health care); substance use; risky behaviours (for example, injecting drugs); experiences of crime and victimisation, and finally a self-assessment of their current needs. The interviews took place in a variety of settings, mainly hostels and day centres, and lasted between one hour and two and a-half-hours.

---

3. See Appendix A for details of services provided by homelessness agencies.
4. Available on request from Dr Emma Wincup, e-mail E.L.Wincup@ukc.ac.uk

Interviews with service providers

In addition 22 semi-structured interviews were conducted with professionals who work with homeless young people. The sample was selected to comprise professionals working in varied settings who had day-to-day contact with homeless young people and included the following types of workers:

- hostel staff (n=6);
- project workers in drop-in housing advice and young people's advice centres (n=4);
- day centre staff (n=4);
- outreach workers (n=3);
- nurses (including one community psychiatric nurse) who work with homeless people (n=2);
- *Big Issue* vendor support worker (n=1);
- young people's services manager (n=1); and
- a supported housing worker (n=1).

The interview schedule was divided into four sections, commencing with questions about their personal characteristics, current post and previous work experience. The following three sections covered their general experiences of working with homeless young people, substance use and health issues.

Limitations of the research

There are a number of potential sources of bias in the sample. With a target sample size of 40 interviews in each area the ability to identify definitive regional differences was limited. Despite the broad definition of homelessness adopted, the sample is unlikely to be a true reflection of the hidden homeless population. Interviewees were contacted via a range of homelessness agencies, obviously excluding those not accessing any homelessness services. The most obvious source of bias was the fact that interviewees choose to participate. The nature of the research meant that sometimes the research team's interest was viewed with suspicion, and although their sustained presence in homelessness agencies was intended to alleviate this, it is likely that some potential interviewees declined to be interviewed as a result. A number of strategies were utilised to encourage participation including the payment of ten pounds to participants and allowing the interviewee to chose the most convenient time to be interviewed. The only group that were excluded were those who were not sufficiently fluent in English. All other young people aged 25 or under in contact with homelessness services were eligible for inclusion.

Structure of the report

The next chapter describes the characteristics of the homeless young people who were interviewed and pathways into, and out of, homelessness. The following four chapters examine: patterns of substance use (Chapter 3); consequences of substance use and homelessness (Chapter 4); accessing services and service provision (Chapter 5) and prevention and harm reduction (Chapter 6). The conclusions and a number of specific recommendations are presented in the final chapter.

2.   Sample characteristics and homeless careers

Demographic information

Of the 160 homeless young people interviewed 71 per cent were male and 29 per cent were female. The mean age of interviewees was 20 years: 22 per cent (n=35) were aged between 16 and 17, 39 per cent (n=62) were aged between 18 and 21 and 39 per cent (n=63) were aged between 22 and 25. Women were on average younger than the men (19 compared with 21).

Eighty per cent of the sample were white British (n=128), however, minority ethnic groups were disproportionately represented in the sample in comparison with the general population[5]. The number of minority ethnic interviewees (n=16) was too small to draw any conclusions regarding differences between ethnic groups, which mainly comprised white/black Caribbean (n=3), black African (n=2), black British (n=3), and black Caribbean (n=4). The remainder were predominantly white Irish (n=6) or white Other[6] (n=9).

---

5.   Approximately two per cent of the population aged 10 and over are of black ethnic origin, three per cent of Asian origin and one per cent 'other' non-white ethnic groups (Research, Development and Statistics Directorate, 2000).
6.   These were generally European.

Current living situation

Table 2.1:   Current living situation by sex

Current living situation	% males (n=113)	% females (n=47)	% of sample (n=160)
Hostel for young people	30	45	34
Street	20	9	16
General hostel[1]	15	2	11
Night shelter	15	2	11
Accommodation with support	10	23	14
Friends	5	6	6
Family	4	9	6
Other[2]	1	2	1
Squat	0	1	1
Total[3]	100	99	100

Notes:
1. These hostels accept people aged 18 or over. There is no maximum age.
2. One young person was living in bed and breakfast accommodation and the other in a drug rehabilitation project.
3. Where totals in this table and throughout the report do not equal 100% differences are due to rounding.

Table 2.1 shows the living situation of the young people at the time they were interviewed. Both men (30%) and women (45%) were most commonly living in hostels for young people. Men were far more likely than women to be living in a night shelter or a general hostel. Almost one-fifth of the young men were living on the streets compared with only nine per cent of young women. Young women were more likely to be living in accommodation with support. There were also important differences between age groups. The majority (57%) of those aged 16 and 17 were living in hostels for young people compared with 40 per cent of those aged between 18 and 21 and only 16 per cent of those aged between 22 and 25. Sixteen to twenty-one-year-olds were also more likely to be living in accommodation with support, than older interviewees. Sleeping on the street was most common among 22 to 25-year-olds (25%) compared with 13 per cent of those aged between 18 and 21 and 6 per cent of 16 and 17-year-olds (n=2).

Stability of current living arrangements[7]
The instability of living arrangements was highlighted by the fact that the majority of those interviewed (80%) had lived in their current situation for less than six months (see Table 2.2). Forty-three per cent had lived there for less than one month, of whom over one-third had

---

7.   This refers to occupying some form of accommodation and rough sleeping.

lived there for one week or less. Furthermore, almost a quarter of the sample (23%) did not know how long they expected to remain living where they were at the time of the interview (see Table 2.3). A further quarter of the sample expected to continue where they were for less than a month, and over one-third (35%) of these expected to stay for less than a week.

Table 2.2: *Length of time young people had spent in current situation*

Length of time lived in current situation	% of sample (n=160)
One week or less	16
One week to one month	27
One to three months	9
Three to six months	28
Six to twelve months	11
One to two years	5
Over two years	5
Total	101

Table 2.3: *Length of time young people expected to continue living in current situation*

Length of time expect to continue living in current situation	% of sample n=160
One week or less	9
One week to one month	16
One to two months	11
Two to six months	17
Six to twelve months	9
Over one year	14
Don't know	23
Total	99

Risk factors

A background of being in care has been identified as a potential precursor for homelessness (Randall, 1998). Almost two-fifths (39%) of the sample had been looked-after by the local authority, including foster care. Seventeen per cent of the young people had become homeless once these care arrangements ended and others had not managed to sustain tenancies subsequent to being looked after. Another risk factor for homelessness is a history of institutional living (Randall, 1998), and experiences of living in institutions were common. Over one-third (35%) had been in prison or a young offender institution, and five per cent had been in a mental health institution. One-fifth had experience of living in at least two of these situations. Forty-three per cent of the sample had not experienced any form of institutional living.

Becoming homeless

The age at which the young people became homeless for the first time ranged between 11 and 25, with a mean age of 17. Of particular concern is the finding that 28 per cent of the sample became homeless[8] before the age of 16. This has major implications for young people. Service provision is predominantly limited to young people aged over 16, with only a small number of voluntary sector projects being prepared to work with young homeless people under 16. In the UK a young person must be in the care of a parent, guardian or social service department up to the age of 16, and if found by the police young people have to be returned home or to substitute care. For these reasons young people often try to remain invisible and find themselves without access to most homelessness services.

The young people interviewed were asked to identify whom they were living with before they became homeless, and the type of accommodation they were living in. The most frequent response was living with parent(s) in the family home (n=89), followed by guardian (n=27), which included young people being 'looked-after' by the local authority. Fifteen of the sample (9%) stated that they were living alone, 12 (8%) said with a partner and four (3%) with friends. All those living alone, with friends or with partners were occupying accommodation rented from a private landlord, city council or housing association. Eight per cent of the sample indicated that they were living with a family member, other than their parents, in their homes.

Childhood experiences of running away from home can be a precursor to later periods of homelessness (Ravenhill, 2000). Fifty-eight per cent (n=93) of the sample answered yes to the question 'before you were 16 did you ever run away for a period longer than a day?'[9] The median number of times they had run away from home was four. The vast majority (n=82) of those who stated that they had run away from home could be classified as 'serial runaways' (Lawrenson, 1997). These young people had established patterns of running away, usually to escape abuse or rejection, with a danger of drifting into homelessness, prostitution or residential or substitute care.

8. This group of people had run away and remained homeless. It does not include young people under 16 who became homeless with their families.
9. This included before they were homeless if they became homeless for the first time aged 15 or under.

Given that many of the sample were living with their parent(s) prior to becoming homeless, it is unsurprising that many of the reasons given for homelessness related to the family. The most common explanation offered was family conflict, usually with one or both parents or a step-parent[10] (n=49). Drug and alcohol use was mentioned by 33 interviewees (21%). This was the second most common explanation (see Chapter 4). The third most frequent explanation was experiencing abuse within the family, foster family or children's home (n=32). This fits with the findings of other studies on homeless young people (Carlen, 1996; Hutson and Liddiard, 1994). The agency staff interviewed offered similar explanations.

As well as explaining their reasons for leaving home, the young people described the manner in which they left. In some instances the young people chose to leave, although it must be recognised that in many cases their choices were constrained ones. Their departures were rarely planned and they had sometimes left suddenly because of a specific instance such as an argument or violent episode. In other cases, they were 'forced' to leave, sometimes with little notice. The implications for young people were that they often found themselves with nowhere to go, sometimes with little notion of how to access agencies that might be able to help them and lacking awareness of the difficulties of securing accommodation.

Experiencing homelessness

The young people interviewed were able to identify a large number of places in which they had slept. These are illustrated in Table 2.4.

---

10. This excludes conflicts that respondents explicitly related to substance use.

Table 2.4: Typology of accommodation and other sleeping places occupied by the young people as they moved in and out of homelessness

Housing category	Examples
'Semi permanent' accommodation[1]	Rented accommodation; accommodation linked to work; supported accommodation
Informal temporary accommodation	With friends and relatives; with strangers
Formal temporary accommodation	Hostels; bed and breakfasts; night shelters; hotels
Criminal justice and other institutions	Prisons; bail and probation hostels; drug residential rehabilitation centre; hospitals, psychiatric units.
Rough sleeping	Locations include streets, beaches, stairwells and doorways, bin sheds, under piers, in cars, in bus shelters, at train stations; in phone boxes, in dustbins, in public toilets, on roofs and in woods.
Other	Squats; tents; caravan and traveller sites

Note:

1. This category is termed semi-permanent in recognition of young people's relationship with housing which is often insecure because of their actions (for example, getting evicted, often due to rent arrears or simply being unable to cope with tenancies and leaving); the time restrictions placed upon their leases and the general insecurity of the private rented housing market.

The young people interviewed were a heterogeneous group in terms of their relationship with the categories of accommodation described above. Their homeless 'careers' could be categorised in the following ways:ac

1. moving between different forms of temporary accommodation, sometimes spending periods of time sleeping rough;
2. moving between temporary and semi-permanent accommodation, sometimes spending periods of time sleeping rough;
3. staying only in temporary accommodation such as hostels (this group had usually not been homeless for very long, and may have spent a brief period sleeping rough);
4. currently living in rented accommodation with additional support after a period of time spent living in temporary accommodation and/or sleeping rough; and
5. 'entrenched' rough sleepers.

Although their experiences of being homeless were diverse, there were some common experiences. Almost three-quarters of the sample (n=117) had slept rough at some point in their lives. Interviewees were asked to recall the last seven nights and asked whether they had slept rough on any of them. Forty (25%) indicated that they had spent at least one night sleeping rough in the last week, and 13 (8%) had slept rough for the entire week.

Interviewees were also asked about periods of time that they had spent sleeping rough during the last 12 months. Sixty per cent (n=96) of the sample had slept rough at some point in that period. Sleeping rough was often relatively short-lived (38 (40%) of rough sleepers said less than one month). However, over one-third of the rough sleepers had spent considerable amounts of time sleeping rough in the past year: 36 per cent (n=35) between one and six months and 24 per cent (n=23) for over six months.

Pathways out of homelessness

Table 2.5:   *Young people's perceptions of their current needs*

Current needs	% wanting help[1] (n=160)
Finding permanent accommodation	74
Getting into a hostel	20
Getting into a night shelter	8
Money problems	54
Physical health problems	26
Mental health problems	21
Drug problem	23
Alcohol problem	6
Getting state benefits	24
Finding work	61
Other[2]	17

Notes:
1. Interviewees were able to give multiple responses.
2. Other needs identified were education, training and job skills, and help with individual problems such as dealing with social service teams in relation to looked after children; coping with stress, the effects of abuse and relationships; arranging replacements forms of identification and payment for items including vets' bills and car tax.

Table 2.5 illustrates that the most commonly identified need was help to find permanent accommodation. Those who did not state this need tended to be people who already had semi-permanent accommodation or were living in hostels that they could occupy for a considerable length of time (in some cases up to two years in total).

Although accommodation was the most pressing matter for most of the young people, when they were asked about what they would like help with in terms of their current needs, several other issues arose. The data suggest that for many young people pathways out of homelessness require more than accessing permanent accommodation, but also addressing the other problems such as financial difficulties, unemployment and substance use which put them at risk of being unable to sustain tenancies.

The majority of those interviewed were able to discuss their future plans for getting accommodation. They found it easier to state what they wanted but rather more difficult to indicate how they would achieve it. Some interviewees were able to list a number of options that were open to them, whilst others appeared to have no idea about how they would access permanent accommodation. Most young people aspired to have a 'home of their own', which usually meant renting a flat or house that they could occupy alone or with a partner. Most appeared to be relying on accessing housing association or council accommodation, although some interviewees were exploring the possibility of seeking accommodation in the private rented sector. Homeless young people face multiple barriers to renting in the private sector. This was recognised by many of the interviewees, who felt that the realistic options open to them were likely to be bed sits, shared houses or accessing accommodation in cheaper locations.

Most of the young people interviewed appeared to be aware of the difficulties of accessing permanent accommodation. Commonly cited difficulties are listed below.

- Lack of awareness: some young people found it difficult, especially when they first became homeless, to know where to go to get help.
- Waiting lists: to access social housing young people have to negotiate a series of bureaucratic procedures relating to benefits and housing applications. These can be time-consuming and difficult to understand hence some young people give up.
- Lack of accommodation: Interviewees frequently mentioned shortages of social housing and affordable housing in the private rented sector.
- Financial exclusion (limited incomes, high rents, lack of money for advance rent payments and bonds, and previous rent arrears).
- Other forms of exclusion: many landlords are unwilling to let properties to people dependent on benefits.

- Age-related policies: the single room rent policy[11], for example, restricts the amount of rent available through housing benefit for single people under the age of 25 and results in the reluctance of private sector landlords to rent to young people. This was a particular problem in Canterbury and Brighton and Hove where rents are higher than the national average.

- Housing policy: some young people were either deemed ineligible for housing by the local authority or were likely to have to wait a considerable time to access it. This was largely because they were not in priority need[12], had been classified as intentionally homeless or were seeking housing in areas where they did not have a local connection.

---

11. Single room rent is limited to the average local cost of a privately rented non self-contained single room with shared toilets, bathrooms and kitchens. This is irrespective of whether such accommodation is available locally.

12. At the time of the research in England, the following groups qualified for priority need: pregnant women; people with dependent children; people who are vulnerable as a result of old age, mental illness or handicap, physical disability or other special reason; people who are homeless as a result of a disaster, such as a flood or fire. On 31 July 2002 under the Homeless (Priority Need for Accommodation) (England) Order 2002, it was extended to include 16 and 17-year-olds (with exceptions); care leavers aged between 18 and 20 who were looked after, accommodated or fostered by the local authority when aged 16 or 17; people aged 21 or over who are vulnerable as a result of being looked after, accommodated or fostered; people who are vulnerable as a result of fleeing violence or threats of violence; and, people who are vulnerable as a result of spending time in the armed forces or having been in prison or remanded in custody. The meaning of 'vulnerable' has not been statutorily defined and is therefore determined by the local authority. The National Assembly for Wales introduced similar legislation on 1 March 2001, without the requirement to establish vulnerability.

3.   Patterns of substance use

This chapter explores the use of tobacco, alcohol and illegal drugs amongst the young people interviewed, considers the effects of such use and examines the context in which it occurs.

Prevalence of smoking[13]

The vast majority (n=157) of the young people interviewed stated that they had smoked a cigarette at some point in their lives. The age at which the interviewees had first smoked varied between four and 19 with a median age of 12. Almost all (n=151) of those who had smoked at some point in their lives had gone on to smoke on a daily basis, typically aged between 13 and 14. The White Paper Smoking Kills (Department of Health, 1998) noted that people who start smoking at an early age are more likely than other smokers to smoke for a long period of time. They are also more likely to die prematurely from a smoking-related disease such as cancer, heart disease or respiratory illness. Many of the young people interviewed fell into this 'high risk' category: 86 per cent of the sample had tried a cigarette before the legal age at which cigarettes can be purchased, and 78 per cent had become regular smokers before the age of 16.

Respondents were asked a series of questions about their current use of tobacco. Ninety-four per cent of the sample (n=151) were current smokers, and all except one of these individuals smoked every day. Tobacco use by young homeless people interviewed can be compared to 'housed' young people using data from the 2000 General Household Survey (Office of National Statistics, 2001).

Table 3.1: **Prevalence of smoking amongst homeless and 'housed' young people**

Age Group[1]	Homeless Young People (%) (n=160)	'Housed' Young People (%)
16-19	93	29
20-24	96	35

Table 3.1 shows that levels of smoking amongst homeless young people are much higher than amongst young people generally.

13. Smoking is used in this report to describe tobacco smoking unless otherwise indicated.

Patterns of smoking

Data were also collected on the type of cigarettes smoked by the research participants. Just over one-quarter of current smokers (n=41) only smoked ordinary cigarettes, just under one third (n=48) only smoked hand-rolled cigarettes and the remainder smoked both (n=62). Women were more likely than men to only smoke ordinary cigarettes, and men were more likely than women to smoke only hand-rolled cigarettes. This gender difference is consistent with the results of the General Household Survey, although overall homeless young people reported much higher levels of using hand-rolled cigarettes. The most obvious explanation for this is cost. The young people interviewed had limited incomes and the rise in the real price of packaged cigarettes in the past decade means that hand-rolled ones are cheaper. In just over three-quarter of cases (n=85), young people who smoked hand-rolled cigarettes did not use filters, with consequent implications for health. Only four people interviewed restricted their smoking to 'light' (i.e. low tar) cigarettes only, and this is inconsistent with the findings of the General Household Survey. There is a lack of consensus about the health benefits of smoking low tar cigarettes with some researchers suggesting that the health risks may be almost the same as for conventional brands (Jarvis and Bates, 1999).

The young people interviewed were questioned about the number of cigarettes they typically smoked in one day. It is possible that the responses given are an underestimate of cigarette consumption. The General Household Survey reports note that when respondents are asked how many cigarettes a day they smoke, there is a tendency to round down to the nearest multiple of ten. In addition, as smoking becomes less acceptable as a social habit, some people may be less inclined to admit how much they smoke. The amount of cigarettes the young people smoked per day varied considerably. The median number of cigarettes smoked each day was 15, and this was the same for men and women.

Table 3.2:   Daily cigarette consumption

Number of cigarettes smoked per day	% of daily smokers (n=151)
Less than 10	22
10-19	41
20-29	24
30-39	3
40-49	5
More than 50	3
Total	98

Individuals smoking 20 or more cigarettes a day are generally regarded as heavy smokers. Just over one-third (n=53) of daily smokers could be described in this way. Heavy smoking puts them at increased risk of coronary heart disease, stroke and lung cancer.

Almost three-quarters of current smokers (n=110) stated that they sometimes mixed tobacco with illegal drugs. In the majority of these cases (n=101) only cannabis was mixed with tobacco but a small number (n=9) admitted to using other substances such as cocaine.

Prevalence of alcohol use

Methodological issues
As Goddard and Thomas (1999) note obtaining reliable information about drinking is difficult, and surveys record lower levels of alcohol consumption than would be expected from data on alcohol sales. Under-reporting may not be deliberate and reflects the problem of keeping track of how much alcohol has been consumed, particularly if people have been drinking large amounts or drinking at home in non-standard measures. There are a number of ways of obtaining data on drinking patterns. The method used for the research reported here was to ask respondents how often they have an alcoholic drink, to describe how much they had to drink the last time they drank alcohol and then to ask whether this was a typical drinking day.

Frequency of drinking alcohol
With the exception of three interviewees, all those who participated in the research had drunk alcohol at some point in their lives. Those who had not drunk alcohol at all were asked why. Two suggested that it was because of concerns they had about the impact of drinking on their physical and/or mental health, and the third had witnessed the impact of her father's heavy drinking and had vowed never to drink.

The age at which they had their first proper alcoholic drink[14] varied between two and 21, with a mean age of 13[15].

---

14. This is defined as 'having a whole drink to yourself rather than a sip'.
15. In England and Wales it is permissible for children aged from five upwards to consume alcohol in private settings such as their homes but not on licensed premises.

Table 3.3:   Frequency of drinking alcohol by gender

Frequency of drinking alcohol	% of females (n=47)	% of males (n=113)	% of the sample (n=160)
Every day	13	8	9
Almost every day	13	9	10
About twice a week	11	14	13
About once a week	11	19	16
About once a fortnight	13	19	17
About once a month	11	6	8
Only a few times a year	13	7	9
Never now	15	17	16
Never drunk alcohol	2	2	2
Total	102	101	100

The young people's use of alcohol varied considerably. Whilst nine per cent (n=15) of the sample stated that they drank alcohol every day, 18 per cent (n=29) did not drink at all at the time they were interviewed. Recent research has suggested the drinking patterns of young women are becoming increasingly similar to those of young men (Wright, 1999). This is reflected in the data above, although a slightly higher proportion of women in the sample admitted to drinking every day or almost every day. However, this finding should be treated with caution because of the small number of female research participants. Findings from the General Household Survey (Office of National Statistics, 2001)[16] indicate that three per cent of men and two per cent of women aged between 16 and 24 drink everyday.

Interviewees were also asked to specify what type of alcohol they usually drank. The typical response was either ordinary lager[17] (n=40) or strong lager[18] (n=38). A considerable number (n=20) also stated that they usually drank spirits.

Patterns of alcohol use

The Department of Health's guidance about sensible drinking formerly referred to 21 units per week for men and 14 units per week for women. The latest guidance combines an emphasis on frequency and quantity of consumption. Drinking between three and four units, or fewer per day

---

16.   The General Household Survey asks respondents about the number of drinking days in the previous week.
17.   This is commonly 3.5-4.5% ABV.
18.   Strong here refers to 5-6% ABV lagers such as Stella, rather than super strength lagers (8-9% ABV) such as Special Brew.

for men, and between two and three units or fewer per day for women is unlikely to pose any significant risks to health. However, regular consumption of four or more units per day for men, and three or more units per day for women can lead to an increasing risk to health. The guidance relates specifically to adults, but in the absence of specific advice for under 18s, researchers have often used it to classify young people's drinking (Newburn and Shiner, 2001).

The data gathered provide some information on the quantity of alcohol typically drunk by the young people. Those who had drunk alcohol (n=157) were asked how much they had to drink the last time they drank alcohol; 119 interviewees were able to answer the question and gave a specific response. Their responses included the amount they had to drink and the types of alcohol they had consumed[19]. This provides a reasonable estimate because 65 respondents said that this reflected the amount they usually drank (33 said it was more than usual and 33 said it was less than usual). Seven respondents were unable to remember how much alcohol they had on the last occasion. These were all infrequent drinkers defined for the purposes of this study as people who drank once a fortnight at most, and the last time they drank alcohol may have been some time ago.

Table 3.4: **Alcohol units consumed in the last drinking session by gender**

Gender	Age	Minimum	Maximum	Median
Women				
	16-17	2	63	8
	18-21	1	20	9
	22-25	2	11	3
	Total	1	63	6
Men				
	16-17	2	109	12
	18-21	1	36	8
	22-25	1	44	12
	Total	1	109	11

The most striking finding from Table 3.4 is the contrast between median amount of units drunk for men and women. It appears that even though young women's drinking is becoming similar to young men's on some measures, important gender differences remain. Heavy drinking continues to be particularly, although not exclusively, associated with young men and this is in keeping with data on alcohol consumption amongst young people generally (Newburn and Shiner, 2001).

19.   This was then translated into units by the research team.

Using the data on the last time they drank alcohol, respondents were put into four categories.

Category 1. Those who had consumed three or fewer units (for men) and four or fewer units (for women) i.e. those drinking within sensible drinking limits defined by the Department of Health.
Category 2. Those who had consumed between five and 10 units (for men) and four and seven units (for women) i.e. those exceeding sensible drinking limits with consequent implications for health.
Category 3. Those who had consumed between 11 and 21 units (for men) and eight to 14 units (for women).
Category 4. Those who had consumed more than 21 units (men) and 14 units (women) i.e. those consuming more than the recommended weekly limits in one drinking episode.

Those in categories three and four could be described as binge drinkers. There is little consensus on what the term means (Newburn and Shiner, 2001) and the definition adopted here is drinking half of the weekly recommended units of alcohol in a single drinking session (National Assembly for Wales, 2000a). This has implications for health by increasing the risk of cardiovascular and coronary heart disease. It can also lead to involvement in crime, other forms of anti-social behaviour, unsafe sex and accidents; although no causal relationship can be inferred.

Analysing the data for those respondents who were able to give details of the last time they drank revealed that only 27 per cent of current drinkers had drunk within sensible daily limits on their last drinking occasion. Twenty-three per cent fell into category two, 32 per cent in category three and 18 per cent had consumed more than the recommended weekly amount the last time they drank alcohol. There were some differences related to gender and age.

Table 3.5: *Alcohol units consumed in the last drinking session by gender and relationship with sensible daily limits[1]*

Gender	Age	% Category 1 (n=32)	% Category 2 (n=28)	% Category 3 (n=38)	% Category 4 (n=22)	Total
Women	16-17	27	18	27	27	99
	18-21	31	13	43	13	100
	22-25	71	14	14	0	99
	Total	38	15	32	15	100
Men	16-17	16	23	31	31	101
	18-21	29	26	39	7	101
	22-25	19	29	26	26	100
	Total	22	27	31	20	100

Note:
1. Current drinkers only, excludes those unable to recall how much they had drunk.

Table 3.5 illustrates that women were more likely than men to be drinking within sensible daily limits; however, a similar proportion of men and women could be defined as binge drinkers. The data on drinking patterns for women suggests that when women become older, they moderate the amount they drink. The available data does not illustrate this for men. Research has suggested that marriage, stable relationships and parenthood have all been shown to moderate young men's drinking habits (see Newburn and Shiner, 2001 for an overview). These were rarely features of the lives of the homeless young men interviewed. Whilst a small number were fathers, they were typically not in regular contact with their children.

Problem drinking

For the purposes of this study problem drinking is defined as consuming more than the sensible daily limits (i.e. those in categories 2, 3 or 4) and drinking every day or almost every day. Using this definition 23 people (14% of the sample) can be viewed as problem drinkers. Twelve per cent of current drinkers (n=15) felt that their use of alcohol was a problem but this figure rose to 39 per cent (n=9) amongst those defined by the research team as potentially problem drinkers. Young people regularly exceeding daily sensible limits failed to recognise the problematic nature of their behaviour.

Thirteen per cent of current drinkers (n=17) agreed that they had felt the need for help or treatment in the past in relation to their drinking. Nine of these still identified themselves as problem drinkers. Seven of those who identified their use of alcohol as a problem stated that they did not feel the need to seek help or treatment.

Forty-seven current drinkers (36%) had tried to give up or cut down on their drinking at some point in their lives. The reasons given were diverse. They included:

- health concerns (n=9);
- cost (n=5);
- realising that their drinking was getting out of control (n=5);
- suffering ill-effects (n=3);
- realising that drinking can lead to violent or other offending behaviour (n=6);
- being encouraged by other people in their lives to give up (n=3); and
- no longer being interested in drinking (n=5).

Twenty-three per cent (n=29) of current drinkers suggested that they would like to give up drinking altogether.

Former alcohol users

Twenty-six of the young people interviewed had drunk alcohol in the past, but were no longer drinking when they were interviewed. Only one person mentioned using an alcohol service to give up drinking. Respondents were asked why they chose to give up. The most common reasons were:

- having a bad experience due to alcohol, for example ending up in hospital with alcohol poisoning (n=6);
- realising that drinking can lead to aggressive and violent behaviour (n=5);
- death of a close family member or friend due to alcohol (n=3);
- seeing the impact of heavy drinking on others (n=3); and
- pregnancy (for women) (n=2).

Context of alcohol use

Two questions were asked to explore the situations in which the young people drank alcohol. Firstly they were asked where they typically were when they drank alcohol. The most frequent response was in the pub (n=55) followed by outside (n=30). Those interviewees who stated that they usually drank outside were largely (n=26) made up of rough sleepers and those living in hostels, and this can be explained by having nowhere else to go. Hostels, day centres and night shelters often have 'no alcohol' policies. Whilst this group could drink in a pub this is much costlier than purchasing alcohol from a shop. Secondly the homeless young people were asked who they were usually with when they drank alcohol. Almost three-quarters (n=96) of current drinkers stated that they usually drank with friends with only 18 replying that they drank alone. Altogether this suggests that like other young people drinking alcohol forms part of wider social activities such as meeting with friends (Newburn and Shiner, 2001).

Prevalence of drug use[20]

The lifetime prevalence of drug use amongst the sample was very high (see Table 3.6).

---

20. The young people were asked about the use of each of the drugs included in the BCS in their lifetime, the last year and last month so that the data could be compared with BCS data for young people aged between 16 and 25. In order to gain more detailed information about their current drug use respondents were also asked about their drug use in the last week.

Table 3.6:   *Use of drugs by young people*

Drug	Use of drugs (%) (n=160)			
	Ever	Last year	Last month	Last week
Any	95	89	76	73
Cannabis	94	80	68	53
Amphetamine	73	32	12	6
Ecstasy	64	44	21	13
LSD	54	19	4	1
Magic mushrooms	51	19	4	1
Cocaine	50	34	15	4
Poppers	50	16	8	1
Volatile substances	47	7	1	1
Tranquillisers	46	30	18	8
Heroin	43	30	21	20
Crack cocaine	38	27	18	13
Painkillers	37	22	11	3
Ketamine	24	12	2	0
Unknown pills or powders	23	6	2	1
Smoked unknown substances	23	6	1	0
Methadone	21	16	8	2
PCP (phencyclidine)	14	3	0	0
Anything else	11	5	2	0
GHB (gamma hydroxybutyrate)	6	2	0	0

At least half of interviewees had used cannabis, amphetamine, ecstasy, LSD, magic mushrooms, cocaine and poppers. Whilst levels of use of heroin, crack cocaine and ketamine were lower, they were still disproportionately high compared with young people generally (Ramsay *et al.*, 2001). For example, two in five of the homeless young people had used heroin. In addition, a substantial proportion of interviewees had used tranquillisers, strong painkillers, such as DF118s (dihydrocodeine tartrate) and methadone bought illicitly. Prevalence of use in the last year, last month and last week indicate that for many use of drugs is ongoing rather than experimental. This was particularly the case for cannabis, heroin, crack cocaine, ecstasy and tranquillisers.

Table 3.7:   Lifetime use of drugs in comparison with the British Crime Survey

Drug	% ever used	
	Young homeless (n=160)	BCS
Any	95	51
Cannabis	94	45
Amphetamine	73	22
Ecstasy	64	12
LSD	54	11
Cocaine	50	10
Heroin	43	2
Crack cocaine	38	2

Lifetime prevalence rates for use of drugs are generally higher in young people compared with adults (Ramsay et al., 2001). Table 3.7 illustrates that use was considerably more widespread among homeless young people than the BCS 2000[21] population (95% compared with 51%), and this was true for all drugs. Focusing in particular on the use of cannabis, ecstasy, cocaine, heroin, crack cocaine, LSD and amphetamine[22] revealed that there were some similar trends in drug use. Cannabis was the most commonly used amongst both groups followed by amphetamine, ecstasy, LSD and cocaine. Heroin and crack cocaine use is very low in the BCS population. Amongst homeless young people the use of heroin and crack cocaine was high, but lower than that for other drugs.

21.   See Appendix B for details of how the data collection process differed from the BCS.
22.   This was requested by the Drugs and Alcohol Research Unit, Home Office.

Table 3.8: *Use of drugs in the last year in comparison with British Crime Survey*

Drug	Age group (% used)							
	16–17		18–21		22–25		16-25	
	Homeless young people (n=35)	BCS	Homeless young people (n=62)	BCS	Homeless young people (n=63)	BCS	Homeless young people (n=160)	BCS
Any	86	23	86	31	94	28	89	28
Cannabis	80	21	76	29	84	25	80	26
Amphetamine	29	5	31	7	35	6	32	6
Ecstasy	51	5	34	6	49	6	44	6
LSD	26	2	11	4	24	1	19	2
Cocaine	26	1	31	6	43	7	34	5
Heroin	3	0	29	1	46	1	30	1
Crack cocaine	6	0	23	1	43	2	27	1

Comparing rates of drug use in the last year between young people in the sample and the BCS reveals a number of important differences (see Table 3.8). Again the level of use of all drugs was much higher amongst young homeless people, particularly amongst the oldest. Levels of cocaine and ecstasy use were similar amongst young people in the BCS; however, the use of ecstasy was greater than that of cocaine amongst homeless young people, reflecting higher rates of cocaine use amongst affluent young people (Ramsay et al., 2001). By contrast the use of heroin and crack cocaine was more prevalent in less affluent groups of young people in the BCS (see Ramsay et al., 2001), and it is therefore unsurprising that the use of these drugs is more common amongst homeless young people. Socio-economic and lifestyle factors such as unemployment, lack of qualifications, being single and living in rented accommodation also contributed to a greater likelihood of drug use in the BCS (Ramsay et al., 2001). These factors are also common amongst homeless young people and may also explain in part the disparities in rates of drug use between homeless young people and the general population.

With the exception of cannabis, very few young people in the BCS sample had used any drugs in the last month and as a result of this there were few apparent differences in use by age. By contrast amongst homeless young people there were some clear variations (see Table 3.8). Amongst those aged 16 and 17, drug use was generally lower than in older age groups with the exception of ecstasy, cannabis and amphetamine where levels were similar[23]. Levels of crack cocaine and heroin use were particularly low for the youngest group.

23.   Amongst those aged between 18 and 21 the use of cannabis and ecstasy was lower than for other age groups. There are no evident explanations for this and it is therefore likely to be a feature of the sample.

Use of other drugs

In common with studies of substance use amongst young people in general (e.g. Parker *et al.*, 1998), the use of volatile substances (i.e. glues, solvents, gases and aerosols) amongst the homeless young people declined with age over time. By contrast very few of the youngest interviewees had used strong painkillers (n=8) and tranquillisers that had not been prescribed for them (n=6), ketamine (n=2) and PCP (n=1), and none had used GHB or methadone. Those that had used these drugs recently tended to be older.

Gender differences

Drug use is generally more prevalent in men than women (Ramsay *et al.*, 2001) although this difference may be decreasing (Goddard and Higgins, 2001). Nevertheless, among the sample women were just as likely to have ever used a drug as men. Women did, however, report considerably lower use of drugs than men for every drug except cannabis; the most commonly used drug, for which levels were similar. These differences were most apparent for the use of amphetamine (80% men and 57% women), cocaine (57% men and 34% women), ecstasy (71% men and 49% women), heroin (50% men and 26% women) and LSD (64% men and 32% women).

Age of onset

Early age of onset of drug use, particularly before the age of 15, is a risk factor for future problem drug use (Lloyd, 1998)[24]. Figure 3.1 shows that the range of ages at which each drug was first tried varied considerably; several young people began to consume drugs at a very young age, the youngest being aged five. The mean age of initiation to each drug indicates that cannabis and volatile substances were first used at age 14, whereas amphetamine, ecstasy, LSD, magic mushrooms and poppers were on average first tried at the age of 16. Class A drugs associated with dependence such as crack cocaine and heroin were generally first used later at the age of 18 or 19. There was little gender difference in the average age of use of each drug: however, those that used at very young ages tended to be male.

---

24. The average age of onset has recently fallen to 13 (Department of Health, 2002)

Figure 3.1: Age of onset of drug use

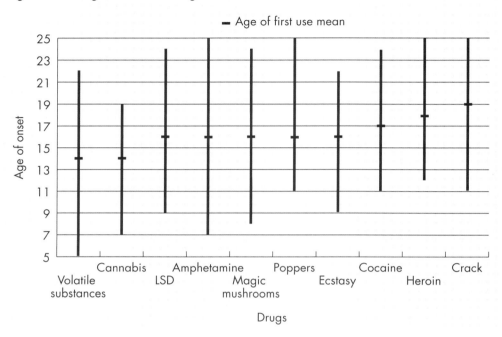

Figure 3.2 illustrates that large proportions of interviewees began to use drugs recreationally, in particular volatile substances, cannabis, magic mushrooms and LSD before the age of 15, indicating that many homeless young people are at risk of future problem drug use.

Figure 3.2: Use of drugs before the age of 15

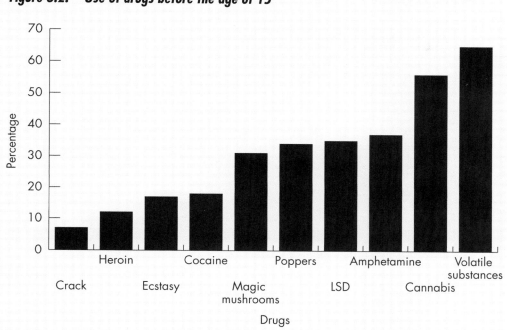

Patterns of drug use

Amongst young people 'the negotiation of drug use and non-use is an ongoing process' (Measham *et al.*, 1998: 10). Similarly, patterns of drug use amongst homeless young people are complex and defining them by their current drug use is therefore simplistic. Nevertheless, the following typology describes the drug using status of young people at the time of interview.

A. Non users
B. Former experimenters
C. Former recreational users
D. Former problem users
E. Current occasional recreational users
F. Current habitual recreational users
G. Current recreational users formerly problem users
H. Current problem users
I. Current problem users in treatment

Current non-users (categories A - D)

Non-users (A)

Those young people (n=8) who had never used drugs were asked to explain why. Non-users had seen the effects of drug use by family and friends or had decided that they did not want to use drugs after being recounted the effects by friends. The remainder viewed drugs as dangerous or they were unfamiliar with them and they therefore did not want, or were too scared, to take them. A further three young people were also classified as non-users. One had not used illegal drugs but had experimented with volatile substances. In addition, two young people had used cannabis but were unaware of what they were taking at the time[25].

Former users (B – D)

Twenty per cent of interviewees had not continued to use drugs. However, this was not necessarily indicative of permanent cessation of drug use. For example, nine former users had taken drugs in the last month indicating that they had only recently stopped using drugs, or used drugs infrequently. Twenty-three (71%) had used drugs in the last year. The term 'former' is therefore used with caution to describe this group. Those that were not currently using could be classified in the following ways.

- Former experimenters (B) (n=8): experimented occasionally, mainly with cannabis but found they did not like its effects.
- Former recreational users (C) (n=17): used drugs such as amphetamine, cannabis, LSD, ecstasy, magic mushrooms and poppers (occasionally also heroin, cocaine and crack cocaine). They gave up for the following reasons: bored with drug taking; and discovering that their drug use put their education achievements, access to housing, relationships (with friends, family or partner) or pregnancy at risk. They also mentioned experiencing imprisonment or violence as a consequence of drug use, lack of money, and concerns about their physical and mental health.
- Former problem users (D) (n=7): defined their former use of drugs such as heroin and crack cocaine as problematic but stopped because they wanted to change the way they lived, for example to become a parent or get employment.

Five young people had stopped temporarily and indicated that they may use again: for example, one had been recently released from prison and one was pregnant.

---

25. These two people had been handed a hand-rolled cigarette, which they thought only contained tobacco, would not have chosen to smoke cannabis and had not used it since.

Current users (categories E – I)

Seventy-three per cent (n=117) of interviewees had continued to use drugs. All except 13 had used drugs in the last week. Cannabis was used most commonly (53%), followed by heroin (20%), ecstasy (13%) and crack cocaine (13%). Cocaine, amphetamine, tranquillisers and other drugs had been used to a lesser extent. One young person had recently used volatile substances. Three young people had used prescribed methadone[26] daily and are therefore described as in treatment. However, two of these had continued to use other substances, including heroin.

The frequency with which drugs were used varied considerably. Users of heroin, crack cocaine and cannabis tended to use these drugs daily, whereas other drugs such as ecstasy, amphetamine, painkillers, tranquillisers and poppers were generally used only on one or two days.

- Current occasional recreational users (E) (n=42): had not used any drugs in the last week or had used drugs such as cannabis, ecstasy and amphetamine (in some cases crack cocaine and heroin) on fewer than five days in the last week.
- Current habitual users (F) (n=32): had used drugs such as cannabis, ecstasy and amphetamine recreationally on five or more days in the last week.
- Current recreational users, formerly problem drug users (G) (n=15): had stopped using drugs such as amphetamine, crack cocaine, heroin and cocaine but continued to use different drugs recreationally.
- Current problem drug users (H) (n=27): had used crack cocaine or heroin on five or more days in the last week, or were using prescribed methadone daily and continuing to use heroin, crack cocaine or cocaine.
- Current drug users in treatment (I) (n=1): had used prescribed methadone daily in the last week.

Problem drug use

Twenty-six per cent of current users felt that their drug use was problematic. For the purpose of this study problem drug use was defined as using heroin, crack cocaine or cocaine on five or more days in the last week, or using prescribed methadone daily and continuing to use heroin, crack cocaine or cocaine. Twenty-seven young people were identified as problem drug users according to this definition. All had defined their use of drugs as a problem, with the exception of one who had cut their drug use down to a minimum in order to access treatment. The definition adopted above excluded four young people who identified their drug use as problematic. Two of those who were excluded had used heroin on two days of the last week. The remaining two had used several drugs recreationally in the last week.

26.   This includes both oral and injectable methadone.

A further 23 young people identified themselves as former problem users or could be identified by the research team as such. This included the seven people who had stopped using drugs altogether, 16 young people who had continued to use drugs recreationally but had been problem drug users in the past and one young person who was adhering to treatment.

Characteristics of problem drug users

The key characteristics of both former and current problem users were defined as those exhibited by 13 or more of current problem users. These are detailed in Table 3.9.

Table 3.9: Key characteristics of problem drug users

Characteristic	% of current problem users[1] (n=27)	% of former problem drug users (n=23)[2]
Male	78	74
White	96	96
Reported family conflict	85	74
Slept rough	78	87
Ran away	56	70
Diagnosed with depression or other mental health problem	52	57
Experienced imprisonment	63	70
Lower than average age of onset of drug use	59	70
First used heroin after homeless[3]	48	48
First used crack cocaine after homeless[4]	63	52
Consider drug use a problem	96	0
Want help to access treatment	96	0
Accessed treatment in past	93	39
More than one attempt to give up	81	Not known[5]
Prioritise spending money on drugs	74	4
Currently injecting	74	0
Consider offences to be related to drug use	89	70

Notes:
1. Interviewees were able to give multiple responses.
2. This also includes young people who had described their use of cocaine and amphetamine as problematic, some of whom had not used heroin or crack cocaine.
3. This was calculated using the age when the young person first became homeless and the age when they first used heroin. It is likely to be an underestimate because those young people who used heroin in the same year that they became homeless are not included.
4. This was calculated using the age when the young person first became homeless and the age when they first used crack cocaine. It is likely to be an underestimate because those young people who used crack cocaine in the same year that they became homeless are not included.
5. Detailed accounts of former problem users experiences of giving up were not requested.

In common with the sample as a whole, problem users were predominantly white and male. The majority had slept rough but were not typically doing so at the time of interview, particularly former problem users. A large proportion reported family conflict and had run away before becoming homeless. The group also displayed high levels of diagnosed mental health problems. The age at which drug use commenced was in general below the average for the sample as a whole (i.e. 14). However, many had not used heroin (48%) or crack cocaine (58%) until after they became homeless.

The vast majority of current problem users wanted help to access help or treatment. Many had accessed treatment in the past on at least one occasion. Three-quarters of current users admitted to prioritising spending money on drugs over other items. It is interesting to note that amongst former problem drug users who had continued to use drugs recreationally this was no longer a financial priority. Most problem drug users admitted that they had committed offences related to their drug use and many of them had been in prison as a result.

Giving up and cutting down

Sixty-eight per cent (n=103) of those who had used a drug had tried to give up or cut down at least once. The reasons for such decisions varied, but the most common response (n=22) was that they wanted to get their lives 'sorted out'. More specific explanations included cost, health or mental health concerns, the influence of non-drug using peers and feeling that their drug use was out of control. Current problem users did not differ greatly from non-problem users in their motivations for curtailing drug use. Twenty per cent of those who had ever used drugs said they had stopped at the time of the interview: however, for a substantial proportion this had occurred only relatively recently (see page 34). The explanations given by this group for stopping have already been outlined. Several current users, including nine problem users, stated that they had recently slowed down their use, some in preparation to stop. Strategies to modify their drug use had been developed by some young people, for example, keeping away from drug using friends and peers in order to make abstinence easier.

Almost half (n=53) of current users would like to give up drug use altogether and a further two per cent (n=2) did not know whether they would. A high proportion of current users stated that they would find it very or fairly difficult to go without drugs for a week (45%) or a day (28%), suggesting that giving up would represent a great test for many (n=56 and n=32 respectively). Current users were also asked whether they felt they needed help or treatment for their drug use, and 46 (40%) agreed that they did (see Chapter 5).

Context of drug use

Current users were asked whether they used a regular source of drugs. Eighty-eight (78%) replied that they did. They were also asked where they got the main drug they used from. The majority of young people acquired their drugs through someone they described as a dealer (n=71), but a number of other sources were identified including friends (n=30), relatives (n=6) and people on the street (n=2).

The majority (69%) of young people who were taking drugs at the time of the interview usually did so with friends or partners. Three interviewees made the distinction that they took drugs with acquaintances rather than friends, generally other homeless people. A small number of young people (n=8) took drugs with family members, primarily siblings and cousins, but also parents, aunts and uncles. Almost one-fifth of young people (n=21) reported that they often took drugs alone, with potentially greater risks to their safety, although the young people did not explicitly state this. Eighty-three (79%) of those that took drugs with other people generally used the same drug as the people they were with.

Interviewees were asked to assess how their levels of drug use equated with people that they spent time with on a typical day i.e. their peers. Only 21 (18%) thought that levels of drug use amongst their peers were lower than their own. However, over one-third (n=43) thought that it was more. The remainder thought that their level of drug use was much the same as others (n=47) or stated that it varied (n=6). Over one-fifth (n=34) of young people had felt under pressure to take drugs, primarily from friends (n=20), but in a small number of cases from other users of homelessness agencies (n=2), dealers (n=2) and ex-partners (n=3). Discussions with young people regarding why they first took drugs indicated that their initiation into drug use, or introduction to the use of particular drugs, often occurred when they were offered them in a peer group situation. Some young people found that they had taken drugs such as heroin, crack cocaine and cocaine that they would not have chosen to use because they were offered what they thought, or were told, was cannabis mixed with tobacco.

The young people were asked whether they were usually inside, outside, in public toilets or anywhere else when they took drugs[27]. Forty-seven (41%) said they were usually inside. A slightly lesser proportion (n=45) stated that they usually took drugs anywhere and a further 16 were outside. The remainder took drugs both inside and outside (n=6) and in two cases were usually in public toilets. The young people interviewed made judgements regarding the location of their drug use. Eighty-three per cent (n=95) of young people identified places that they avoided taking drugs, detailed in Table 3.10.

27.   The wording of this question was structured to avoid disclosure of drug use on the premises of homelessness services that contravened the Misuse of Drugs Act 1971 and was requested by one service provider.

Table 3.10: Typology of places avoided when taking drugs

Places avoided	% avoided taking it there[1] (n=95)
In public e.g. parks, town centres	47
Homelessness agencies e.g. hostels, day centres, *Big Issue* offices	27
Criminal justice agencies e.g. police station[2], courts	25
Other people's houses e.g. parents, non-drug using friends	13
Public toilets	11
Round children	11
Other outside locations e.g. near CCTV, festivals	7
Other inside locations e.g. work, hospital, squat	6
Social venues e.g. pubs, clubs	5
Drugs agencies	1

Notes:
1. Interviewees were able to give multiple responses.
2. This answer was repeatedly given as a joke!

These decisions reflected a desire to:
- hide drug use from others to avoid arrest or revealing their use to others;
- not expose non-drug users;
- compromise the position of agencies, or risk exclusion by contravening the rules;
- avoid vulnerability to accidents when under the influence; and
- avoid specific locations where they felt drug use was not appropriate.

Poly-drug use[28]

Ninety-five current users identified one or more drugs that they particularly liked to use; some could not make a preference for one drug in particular and therefore mentioned several (n=14). Furthermore, 22 respondents would use something else if they were unable to obtain their drug of choice. Fifty-five current users (47%) had used more than one drug in the last week. This indicates that many homeless young people take a range of drugs.

The regular use of several drugs, particularly concurrently or consecutively, can exacerbate the risks posed to health. Fifty-nine per cent (n=69) of current drug users sometimes used more than one drug, including alcohol, at the same time. Respondents were asked which drugs they mixed and why they mixed them. A variety of drugs were used simultaneously

28. Concurrent or consecutive use of more than one illicit substance, alcohol and/or non-medical use of pharmaceuticals' (European Monitoring Centre for Drugs and Drug Addiction, 1999: 90)

with others: however, heroin and cannabis were those most commonly mixed with other drugs. While 64 per cent of young people only used two substances simultaneously on any one occasion, a quarter used several drugs in combination, and 12 per cent were unable to specify how many or which drugs they mixed.

Drug using behaviour

Current users were asked whether they took any steps to ensure that their drug use was as safe as possible. These are detailed in Table 3.11.

Table 3.11: *Typology of measures taken to ensure drug use was as safe as possible*

Measures taken	% of current users[1] (n=117)
Safe using e.g. only 'safe' drugs, water with ecstasy, not injecting, limit amount	47
Safe injecting e.g. use own paraphernalia, not injecting in groin, clean needles	22
Safe company e.g. with people known to them, with people who know what they have taken	16
Safe buying e.g. know who they are buying from, know what drugs they are buying	13
Examination of drug or its effects e.g. check it, use from a batch that has been around for a while, see effect on others first	10
Safe environment e.g. clean, familiar	6

Note:
1. Interviewees were able to give multiple responses.

The assumptions made by young people that their drug use practices were safe were in some cases questionable, for example knowing the drug vendor. Furthermore 13 per cent took no safeguards, some (primarily those that only used cannabis) because they did not feel that the drugs they used required it.

Injecting behaviour

Just over a quarter of the sample (n=42) had used drugs intravenously. Over half of these (55%) had injected in the last four weeks (n=23). All recent injectors had injected with heroin, and eight had additionally injected crack cocaine. One had also used amphetamine and cocaine intravenously.

Current intravenous drug users (IDUs) were asked about where they were on the last occasion that they injected. Over half were inside, but some young people were either outside (17%) or in public toilets (30%), with potentially greater risks for both their safety and the safety of others, for example as a result of discarded needles. Injecting in public places is often related to other risky injecting behaviours including using excessive quantities of drugs, injecting frequently, sharing equipment and overdose (Klee and Morris, 1995). The vast majority (90%) of IDUs did display some regard for safety. The most common locations that they avoided injecting were public places (n=14), outside (n=3), in public toilets (n=4) and around children (n=2). Homelessness agencies (n=6) and other people's houses (n=3) were also mentioned.

Although levels of injecting were high, 87 per cent had used a needle exchange in the last month, indicating a good regard for the use of clean needles and the safe disposal of used needles. IDUs were asked whether they had engaged in risky behaviours such as the sharing of needles or syringes and injecting paraphernalia such as spoons, filters and water. Levels of using a needle or syringe after someone else had used it were fairly low (13%): however, twice as many admitted to passing on a needle or syringe to someone else after they had used it. Forty per cent of those who had injected in the last four weeks had shared paraphernalia such as spoons, filters or water (n=9). Those who had shared had done so with a partner, friends and acquaintances and in one case with anyone. This indicates that although homeless young people appear on the whole not to share injecting equipment, unsafe injecting practices continue to occur. Three ex-users admitted to sharing injecting equipment in the past.

Most drug users who inject believed at one time that they would never inject and the decision to first inject can be a result of seeing others do so (Hunt *et al.*, 2001). The young people were therefore asked about their exposure to injecting by others. Forty-eight (41%) of those that had never injected had encountered injecting, and all stated that they would never inject.

Overdose

Just under a quarter (n=35) of those that had used drugs had overdosed[29] on drugs. Heroin was the most frequently identified cause of overdose: however, small numbers of young people reported overdosing on LSD, ecstasy, crack cocaine, amphetamine, cannabis and caffeine tablets. A high proportion (65%) of those that had overdosed had been to casualty

---

29. Overdose was not defined in the interview. Responses are therefore based on individual interpretation of the term and are likely to include both intentional and accidental overdose.

as a result, indicating willingness to access emergency health services without fear of sanction. Levels of exposure to overdose were high amongst the young people. Over one-third (n=59) had been with people who had overdosed on drugs, and 97 (61%) knew someone who had died as a result of overdose.

4.   Consequences of substance use and homelessness

It is difficult to identify clearly the effects of homelessness on the lives of young homeless people as distinct from the effects of substance use. Factors common to both these issues, such as physical and mental health and offending behaviour, were therefore discussed with interviewees within the context of both homelessness and substance use. The relationship between substance use and homelessness is also considered.

Becoming homeless and substance use

Young people were asked why they thought they had become homeless. Substance use was often one of a plethora of reasons offered (19%). Drug use was more frequently mentioned than alcohol use with 23 interviewees mentioning drugs only, six alcohol only and two both. Typically involvement in substance use had led to the young person being asked to leave the family home. The above finding needs to be qualified further. The data suggest also that the substance use mentioned was often not problematic. If family relationships were fragile discovering that the young person was smoking cannabis was sometimes the ultimate reason for them to be asked to leave. More detailed analysis of current problem users suggested that 48 per cent (n=13) of them were problem drug users when they became homeless[30] or that their drug use was problematic in the sense that it was one reason for their homelessness.

Impact of homelessness on substance use

Interviewees were asked to describe how their substance use had changed since they became homeless. The impact of becoming homeless on young people's use of alcohol varied tremendously. The typical response was that their use of alcohol had stayed the same, either through drinking at the same level (n=63) or continuing not to drink (n=17). Similar proportions felt they began drinking more (n=27) or had begun to drink less (n=26). For ten young people a period of homeless had provided them with an opportunity to give up straightaway. Eight respondents explicitly mentioned becoming a problem drinker and then giving up or cutting down. Five young people mentioned that they began drinking alcohol after they became homeless. For those who stated that they drank less, the reasons

---

30.   Using the definition adopted for the research.

given were typically related to having a very low income. For those who stated that they had begun to drink more, a variety of reasons were offered and these included having more freedom to drink, mixing with young people who were heavy drinkers, wanting to forget their problems and to keep warm when sleeping rough.

Whilst for almost half of those who had previously used drugs homelessness had no impact on their use, many noted changes. Patterns of use after becoming homeless varied considerably but can be broadly classified as follows:

- used drugs more frequently (n=29);
- used a greater variety of drugs (n=11) ;
- used drugs less frequently (n=16);
- increased the frequency or variety of drugs used, then decreased again (n=8).

Increases in the frequency or variety of drugs used were attributed to a range of factors including changes in company kept, increased availability or boredom. Changes also reflected their need to relax, stay awake when sleeping rough, to protect themselves or forget their problems. A small number stated that being homeless had led to them becoming more dependent or beginning to inject. Problem users in particular said they had used a greater variety of drugs since they became homeless. The minority for whom drug use became less frequent cited reasons such as lack of money, less availability, becoming more responsible and a desire not to become addicted.

The vast majority (n=27) of those who were no longer using drugs had stopped during the time they had spent homeless. All except one of those who had been problem users in the past (n=22) had stopped using drugs, or had given up drugs they found problematic, since they became homeless; two had done so whilst in prison and two whilst in treatment. This suggests that an episode of homelessness can provide an opportunity to give up using drugs.

One-fifth of young people were homeless before they ever used a drug and for one young person drug use and homelessness began at the same time. These young people reported that they began to use drugs after they became homeless predominantly because they were exposed to drugs for the first time or drugs were more available to them and they wanted to experiment, or in one case felt pressured into using them. Other reasons cited were related to the use of drugs to achieve particular effects, for example, forget problems, calm down or increase confidence.

Over half of those who had used heroin (n=37) and crack cocaine (n=34) first used them after they became homeless. Furthermore, 18 per cent (n=12) of heroin users and 14 per cent (n=8) of crack cocaine users had used these drugs in the same year that they became homeless, so it can be reasonably assumed that for some this use occurred after homelessness. Current and former problem drug users showed similar patterns. By contrast 114 (77%) of those who had used cannabis first used it before they became homeless and 25 (17%) had used it in the same year.

Providers thought it perhaps unsurprising that homeless young people became involved in drug use. They referred to how it could be seen as a means of escape, or of numbing pain, and also related it to their perception that drug use has now become a key feature of the adolescent landscape in wider society – increasingly prevalent, and even mainstream. Providers also noted that illegal drugs were easy for most young homeless people to obtain. In terms of service delivery, providers found that some levels of drug and alcohol use impeded effective engagement and work with young people. The most chaotic substance users were also those who were least likely to get re-housed, let alone to be housed only to have tenancies fail.

Health

Homelessness has been implicated in causing, maintaining and exacerbating physical and mental health problems (Grenier, 1996). *Saving Lives: Our Healthier Nation* (Department of Health, 1999) highlighted the need to reduce health inequalities related to homelessness and poor housing. The high levels of current use of alcohol, tobacco and drugs by the young people interviewed indicates that reducing such inequalities must be coupled with a consideration of the effects of substance use on health.

Interviewees were asked to describe the state of their general health[31]. Almost half of the sample (46%) described themselves as very healthy or moderately healthy. Over one-third (37%) thought they were of average health, and the remaining 16 per cent saw themselves as unhealthy or very unhealthy.

---

31. It is important to note that people are likely to describe their state of health as better than it is in reality (Cornwell, 1984).

Physical health

Interviewees were asked whether they had experienced physical health problems since they became homeless. Over half of the sample (n=74) had not experienced any physical health problems in this time. Eighty per cent (n=59) of those who had experienced health problems thought that these were related, at least in part, to their homelessness. It is evident that young people understood their state of health to be influenced by a variety of other factors. For example, one-fifth attributed their health problems solely to substance use. Family background and childhood were also commonly cited. Regardless of how the problems initially materialised, interviewees felt that their health was affected negatively by homelessness and substance use.

The incidence of health problems amongst rough sleepers is particularly high (Bines, 1994). This was reflected in perceptions of general health and the health problems experienced by both young people who had slept rough in the past and those that were currently rough sleeping. For example, young people who had not slept rough in the last week were almost twice as likely to describe themselves as healthy than those who had. These differences were also reflected in the higher levels of health problems reported by those who had slept rough.

The health problems experienced by the young homeless people were diverse and reflects those found in other studies (Bines, 1994; Grenier, 1996). These include infectious diseases e.g. coughs, colds and flu; respiratory problems; skin conditions; back and joint problems; infestations e.g. body lice, head lice, ringworm and fleas; wounds and injuries; stomach problems; specific medical conditions e.g. diabetes, sickle cell anaemia, polio, cancer and anorexia; and fits and blackouts.

The young people were asked to describe the difficulties they faced in keeping healthy and the majority of the sample (69%) identified at least one issue. The most common problem discussed was eating adequately (59%). The young people tended to rely on homelessness services to provide food, which was often only once a day. Low income and an inability to store foods also hindered the ability of young people to eat sufficiently (see also Evans and Dowler, 1999). Although most day centres provide washing and laundry facilities, another common problem, mainly for those sleeping rough, was keeping clean. Other difficulties included lack of shelter, warmth, sleep and exercise. Accessing health care was rarely mentioned as an issue for the homeless young people when discussing the difficulties they had in keeping healthy.

When asked how their health problems affected their life many young people stated that they did not. Service providers took the view that some young people prioritised more immediate needs over health, including finding accommodation, and for problem users, obtaining drugs or alcohol. This implies that it is often motivation and prioritisation rather than access to services that is the problem. Grenier (1996) suggested that this form of self-neglect can be a manifestation of a mental health problem, including depression or very low self-esteem, and can also be linked to substance use. Young people were asked to identify their main items of expenditure. Whilst food was stated by over half of interviewees, substance use was also often cited; one-third mentioned drugs, one-fifth mentioned alcohol and one-tenth mentioned tobacco. A quarter of young people admitted to prioritising buying drugs or alcohol over food with consequent implications for health.

Most providers thought that housing homeless young people could in itself significantly improve health. They also stressed that the vast majority of the young people were poorly prepared for independent living (e.g. they often lacked money management or food preparation skills), and without some continued support once re-housed, their levels of health may suffer as a consequence, or at best fail to improve.

Physical health and substance use

Interviewees who were currently using tobacco, alcohol and drugs were asked a series of questions about their perceptions of the impact of this on their health.

Whilst approximately three-quarters of current smokers felt that smoking had affected their health, fewer (approximately half) had concerns about the effects of smoking on their health. The most common ways in which smoking was thought to have affected their health was by causing respiratory problems and making them feel unfit so physical exertion was more difficult. The main concerns were getting cancer and health problems caused by damage to their lungs. Twenty-three per cent of alcohol users thought drinking had affected their health in some way, most commonly referring to stomach and liver problems and general feelings of lethargy. A slightly higher proportion (27%) expressed concerns about the impact of drinking on their health, most frequently expressing concerns about becoming an alcoholic and experiencing liver problems.

Half of current drug users (n=58) felt that drug use had affected their health, 37 of whom were also concerned about the effects of drug use on their health. Almost one-fifth of those who had suffered no problems were nevertheless concerned about the effects of drug use on their health. The majority of those who thought their health had been affected identified physical and mental health problems that they accredited to their drug use. Problem users in particular had suffered from vomiting, weight loss, dental problems, collapsed veins and infections. A number of studies suggest that major communicable diseases such as hepatitis

C and tuberculosis are common among homeless injecting drug users (see for example Croft-White and Rayner, 1999). The young people tended to mention physical health problems that were more identifiable and only one young person said they had contracted hepatitis C.

Drug use also impacted more generally on health. Interviewees reported that they felt unfit, run down or lazy as a result of drug use. Where specific problems were not identified young people knew that their health was likely to have been affected by drug use. Some remarked that heroin acted as a painkiller and probably prevented them from feeling the effects of poor health. Concerns indicated recognition of both immediate consequences of drug use and longer-term effects. Immediate considerations included, for example, dying after taking a 'dodgy pill' or accidental overdose, and contracting illnesses such as hepatitis B and C and HIV through injecting. Worries regarding the future impact of drug use included the risk of cancer, heart and lung disease, the fear of dependency, and not recovering from the effects of their current use.

The apparent gap between levels of reported impact on health and reported concerns can be explained in a number of ways. Given the problems faced by young homeless people it may be that concerns about the impact of substance use on health are overridden by more immediate concerns such as finding somewhere to live. Additionally, the young age of the respondents may explain why they were often unconcerned about long-term effects, perhaps because they feel they can give up and prevent future health problems. For some young people there was no reason for them to have concerns about the impact of substance use on their health, particularly alcohol. However, it seems likely some interviewees underestimated the negative effects of irregular binge drinking.

Mental health

The extent of mental health problems amongst the homeless population is disproportionately high (Bines, 1994), including among young people (Craig et al., 1996). Substance use, in particular problem use, and mental health problems often co-exist (Brown et al., 1996). Drug and alcohol use are implicated in causing mental health problems. Substance use may also begin as a means of managing mental health problems, and can itself be defined as a mental health problem.

Only 30 per cent of interviewees stated that they had had neither depression, any other mental health problem nor had concerns about their mental health. When asked whether they had ever been diagnosed with, or concerned about, depression, a large proportion stated that they had been diagnosed with depression (39%) and a further 23 per cent had concerns that they were, or had been, depressed. Over two-thirds had been diagnosed or had these concerns since they became homeless, but this does not necessarily imply that they can be attributed to homelessness.

Over a quarter of the sample had either been diagnosed with (18%), or concerned about (9%), mental health problems other than depression. About half had been diagnosed or had these concerns since they became homeless. The number of mental health problems that had been diagnosed ranged from one to four. The majority had only one condition and 29 per cent had two. The types of mental health problems diagnosed were diverse and were broadly classified according to Mental Health Foundation categorisation (www.mentalhealth.org.uk). These include anxiety; obsessive compulsive disorder; attention deficit hyperactivity disorder (ADHD); mood disorders; eating disorders; personality disorders; psychotic disorders; sleep disorders[32]; stress disorders e.g. stress, post traumatic stress disorder; and attachment disorder.

In a few cases the young people specifically stated that their mental health problem was substance related. For example, they referred to experiencing 'speed psychosis'. Those who expressed concerns about their mental health were not always able to identify a specific condition. Those who were able to, mentioned concerns about paranoia, panic attacks, ADHD, hearing voices, mood swings and schizophrenia. It must be noted that some of these symptoms can also be attributed to the effects of substance use.

Further indicators of mental health are thoughts of, and attempts to commit, self-harm or suicide. Self-harm and suicide are reportedly common in homeless people, particularly among the young (Grenier, 1996; Craig and Hodson, 1998). Almost half of the sample had thought about or tried to self-harm, and in just under three-quarters of cases this had occurred since becoming homeless. A slightly higher proportion had thought about or tried to commit suicide, and again in three-quarters of cases this had occurred since becoming homeless. Seventy-eight per cent (n=57) of those who had thought about or tried to self-harm had also thought about or tried to commit suicide.

---

32. Sleep disorders were not generally seen by the young people as a mental health problem but were mentioned as a difficulty they faced in keeping healthy.

Offending and victimisation

Young people in general report high levels of offending (Graham and Bowling, 1995; Flood-Page et al., 2000). The homeless young people interviewed admitted to very high levels of offending (95%)[33], double the levels found in the most recent Youth Lifestyles Survey (Flood-Page et al., 2000). Interviewees were not asked specific questions regarding victimisation but it is evident from their accounts of their lives that many had themselves been the victims of crime, both before and after becoming homeless (Buckland, 2002).

Thirty-eight (24%) of those who had offended thought that their offences were linked to alcohol. As Deehan (1999) notes, alcohol can be associated with a wide variety of crimes and the relationship is not simple. Alcohol is not always a causal factor in crime but can contribute to, and be associated with, crime. Those young people who felt their offences were linked to alcohol were asked to describe how they perceived the relationship between the two. A small number (n=5) had committed offences which specifically mention alcohol such as being drunk and disorderly or driving over the legal limit. A slightly higher number (n=8) had either stolen alcohol or committed offences to obtain money to purchase alcohol. The most common response was becoming involved in crime because they were drunk, and these typically included acts of violence and criminal damage.

Over half (n=79) of those who had a history of drug use thought that it had a link with their offending. However, many young people who admitted to possessing drugs did not equate this with committing crime. This was particularly the case for those who admitted to possessing cannabis, 42 per cent (n=54) of whom did not relate their offending to drug use, compared with 32 per cent (n=30) of those who had possessed other drugs. For those who linked their drug use to offending the most common explanations included financing drug use and committing violent offences whilst under the influence of drugs. Seventy-eight per cent of problem and former problem drug users felt that their offending was related to their drug use (see page 37). Again the most common explanation for committing acquisitive crimes such as shoplifting, burglary and theft was to obtain money to fund their drug use.

Homelessness, particularly rough sleeping, is frequently cited as a risk factor for offending. One-third (n=50) of young people who had offended thought that their offending was related to homelessness. The most common explanation for offending was the need for food (n=8) or money (n=36), and these can be regarded as 'survival crimes' (Carlen, 1996). Offending was also attributed to the company young people had mixed with since they became homeless (n=3) and breaking and entering to sleep in a car or building (n=5). In some, but by no means all, cases the money may have been needed to purchase drugs.

33.   Two per cent of the sample declined to answer questions on offending behaviour.

5.   Accessing services and service provision

This chapter will consider, from the standpoints of both the young people and service providers, issues of access to homelessness, health and substance use services, and possible solutions to the barriers, which are identified.

Homelessness services

Challenges for homelessness services

The interviews with service providers explored their perceptions of the problems and needs of the young people. The invariable and overriding theme of their responses was the wide range of service provision demanded by the multiplicity and complexity of presented needs. The oft-perceived futility of their situation leaves many young people without any sense of direction or ambition. Providers commented that often this kind of defeatism or fatalism can lead to substance use, particularly when the impact of peer influence is taken into account. Their views reflect those of the Advisory Council on the Misuse of Drugs (1998), which concluded that it was hard to conceive of a situation more encouraging of substance use than homelessness.

Homelessness service staff reported feeling ill-equipped to deal with the problems with which the young people presented them, and recognised the importance of making appropriate referrals to other agencies to address this. One of their main aims was to protect and prevent some young people from slipping into the 'subculture of homelessness', from which they would find it increasingly difficult to escape as time went by.

Alongside the provision of, or facilitating access to, temporary accommodation for young people, homelessness services also serve as a point of access for a wide range of other interventions. The agencies visited, including day centres, operate both formal and informal assessments in order to make appropriate referrals, and/or to make 'personal plans' for their service users.

Accessing homelessness services

The young people were asked which types of temporary accommodation they had ever used. Table 5.1 illustrates that most had used hostels (both general hostels and hostels for young people), day centres, night shelters, and food runs. Fewer had used outreach teams,

Big Issue services, or cold weather shelters. Homeless young women were less likely than men to have used cold weather (28% men and 6% women) and night shelters (58% men and 21% women), outreach teams (45% men and 21% women) and the *Big Issue* (36% men and 15% women).

Table 5.1:   Use of homelessness services[1]

Service type	% ever used (n=160)	% used in the last month (n=160)	% aware of service could use (n=160)	% would use in future (n=160)
Hostel	74	41	86	78
Day centre	61	46	75	71
Food run	53	33	61	68
Night shelter	47	18	65	67
Outreach team	38	21	54	69
Big Issue	29	16	74	52
Emergency bed unit	23	8	31	46
Cold weather shelter	22	3	34	63

Note:
1. Not all services were available at all research sites at the time of interview e.g. cold weather shelters. The emergency bed unit was unique to one research site; providing temporary accommodation for 20 single homeless. It is staffed round the clock and intended for use as an emergency facility.

Rates of service use during the month prior to interview were much lower than lifetime use. This can in part be accounted for by the finding that at the time of interview some young people had no need to access such services. For example, those living in hostels no longer had a need to access services such as day centres or food runs.

The young people appeared to have relatively high levels of awareness of homelessness services. In line with other research (Fountain and Howes, 2002), the comments of both the young people and service providers indicate that the longer the period of homelessness, the greater the knowledge of available services. Service providers were concerned that the youngest, and most recently, homeless might not be coming to their attention as a result of being unaware of what help is available.

Finally, interviewees were asked which services they would use in future. Again, levels of positive responses were high. Many of the young people qualified their answers regarding with comments such as 'I hope I won't have to', or 'only if I really had to'. Eight young people felt use of these services was perceived as a retrograde step (e.g, the young person was living in supported accommodation, from which they hoped to be moved on into their own home). In other cases, this reluctance had much more to do with negative perceptions or experiences of using the different services. Thirty-four young people specifically stated that hostels, night shelters and day centres are unsafe and intimidating places to be because of the behaviour of other users.

The findings reported here suggest that local policies and circumstances have the greatest impact on provision, resulting in some differing responses to youth homelessness and substance use across the four sites. At the time the research was conducted, one site was about to put into operation a local connections policy, which governed access to accommodation services on the basis of a proven prior connection to the area. Young people with local connections to areas with such policies would benefit from the prioritisation of their needs. However, there are considerable implications for service access and provision should such a policy be more widely adopted. Newly resident homeless young people may find it more difficult to access services than currently. A proliferation of this type of policy may serve to highlight differences in service provision between areas, and provide the impetus for each local authority to ensure that they develop sufficient service responses to both homelessness and substance use.

Barriers to homelessness services access

When asked about their experience of using temporary accommodation, the young people praised highly, and were appreciative of, individual workers and some services. The most positive comments were made regarding dedicated young people's services, or outreach and food run services. However, it was evident that the young people felt that there were a number of barriers to them considering, or actually accessing, temporary accommodation, including:

- a dislike or fear of other service users (n=35) e.g. problem drug users and drinkers; people who steal; violent individuals;
- a general lack of awareness of what is available (n=26);
- insufficient bed spaces (n=12);
- restrictive admissions criteria (n=9) e.g. imposing age limits, restricting admission only to men or women;
- dirty and poorly equipped premises (n=8);
- exclusionary rules (n=8) e.g. being unwilling to accept couples or dogs;
- having to pay for food or drink, or unaffordable rents (n=6);
- feeling shame, embarrassment and stigma due to their situation (n=5);

- having to be drug or alcohol-free prior to admission, or on the premises (n=4); and
- having to leave premises during the day (n=4).

The accounts of problem substance users were examined to see the extent to which they felt their substance use was a barrier to accessing accommodation. Only seven out of the 25 problem drug users explicitly stated reasons why they felt their drug use prevented them from finding accommodation. The typical response was to note that they needed to address their drug use before they could even consider finding somewhere more stable to live (n=5). It was also suggested that problem drug use takes up all of an individual's time and money (n=2). None of the problem drinkers identified their use of alcohol as a barrier to finding housing. These figures need further explanation. In some instances the impact of substance use on their lives meant they had not always begun to make plans for getting accommodation and consider potential obstacles. In addition, whilst substance use was not explicitly mentioned by many respondents, the other difficulties they faced such as limited incomes were likely to be influenced by their use of drugs and/or alcohol.

Exclusions and homelessness services

A total of 35 young people (23%) had been excluded from a homelessness service during the past year, although these exclusions were generally temporary and for fixed periods of one week to one month. Sixteen young people attributed these to issues around conflict or disagreement with staff or other service users; sometimes it was acknowledged that the effects of substance use, and alcohol in particular, had played a role in their behaviour. Only a small number had been excluded for drug use (n=6), drinking (n=2) or drug dealing (n=2), and for one young person his exclusion was due to his drug dealer causing damage to the shared house he was living in.

All services had policies in place regarding drug and alcohol use on their premises, typically barring the use of both, and prohibiting attendance when intoxicated. Whilst also serving to protect staff from prosecution under Section 8 the Misuse of Drugs Act 1971[34], these were primarily designed to ensure the safety of staff and service users, and were thought necessary since both drug and alcohol use could 'get in the way' of effective work. Alcohol use on service premises may also be prohibited as a condition of the service licence arrangements, even where some tenants or their visitors are over 18. The policies were also seen as providing a degree of protection for the young people against exposure to drug or problem drinking.

---

34. The amendment to Section 8 has not yet come into force, and will only do so when guidance is issued from the Home Office on how it will be implemented.

The policies and their application were generally described as 'flexible', and exclusions were said by providers to be rare; at worst, services users would usually receive fixed-period bans for breaches. Accommodation providers sometimes interpreted their role as one of helping maintain a tenancy, not stopping people using drugs or alcohol. Thus if a young person was doing well in all other aspects of a tenancy, then it would be more constructive to continue to provide support, alongside relevant specialist input, than to evict and exclude. Different substances were viewed as presenting different problems of management and detection, and any action providers felt compelled to take against service users invariably flowed from issues around their behaviour, rather than the substance use per se. In these terms, alcohol presents most problems.

Providers did not think that there were high levels of substance use on their premises, since by and large the young people understood why the policies existed and generally supported them; as one respondent put it, services were in this sense 'policed by residents'. Although some young people interviewed said that they disliked being unable to use drugs or alcohol whilst on service premises, others also said that this was a situation they preferred, since they wished to have no contact, or to live, with 'junkies' and 'winos'.

The conviction of two managers at the Wintercomfort project for the homeless in Cambridge in 1999, and the recent amendment of Section 8, have caused anxiety and disquiet amongst staff in day centres, hostels and supported housing (Buckland et al., 2002). Workers at homelessness agencies, if they are to avoid the possibility of prosecution, will need to take decisive action to prevent the supply and use of illegal drugs on their premises. They are concerned about the possible consequences of the legislation for their work with homeless drug users[35]. They expressed concern that relationships of trust will be damaged, harm reduction work will be inhibited, and exclusion rates are liable to rise. One provider commented on the irony of the legal situation: 'We are in a way inviting drug users here – because we are inviting homeless people, and many are users'.

Improving access to homelessness services

The young people and service providers were asked how service access might be improved. The young peoples' suggestions included:

- advertising service availability (n=29);
- more funding to expand and improve services (n=18);

---

35. Pending the publication of Home Office guidance, Release (Flemen, 1999) and DrugScope (2000) have issued advice to assist service providers in developing in-house policies.

- more provision open/available during the daytime (n=13); and
- more outreach work (n=6).

Providers echoed these suggestions, and proposed others. Provision which 'takes services and service access to the young people, wherever they are' was repeatedly advocated, most notably in the form of outreach work. There was also strong support for developing further the practice of bringing other provision (e.g. health, education, benefits) to homelessness agencies in the form of regular sessions or surgeries. Respondents also favoured the 'one-stop-shop' approach, which operates in some areas already. The need for continued development of good working partnerships with other agencies, in order to provide a wider range of responses to the multiplicity of needs presented, was seen as central to meeting need. Some agencies were providing training around homelessness issues to professionals in other service areas.

Strong arguments were made that the most effective improvement would be an increase in the amount of dedicated service provision for homeless young people, which would recognise and respond appropriately to their particular needs, and would, centrally, prevent descent into the 'subculture of homelessness' and its attendant risks. Providers want to be able to provide positive experiences and environments. This is viewed as being best achieved in the context of discrete provision; for example, the placement of a newly homeless young person in a hostel alongside older and longer-term homeless people was considered completely inappropriate, raising the possibilities of 'contamination', bullying and exploitation.

Health services

Physical health

Sixty-nine young people (43%) reported having received treatment for physical health problems since becoming homeless. Thirty-nine had been treated by their GP, 10 had been hospital in-patients, 10 had been hospital outpatients, and nine had been treated at hospital Accident and Emergency (A and E) departments.

Descriptions of the ailments that were last treated by GPs and at hospitals respectively do not suggest the inappropriate use of A and E departments which has been found by other research (see for example, Shelter, 2000). A and E departments appeared only to have been used in the vast majority of cases for serious problems, such as the consequences of accidents and fights, drug or alcohol overdose, and suicide attempts.

All the young people were asked where they would go for help if they became ill. Seventy-three per cent (n=116) stated that they would see their GP, and just nine per cent (n=14) said that they would go to a hospital. The remainder mentioned homelessness agencies, friends or parents' houses. Four interviewees were unable to identify anywhere they would go. This finding, taken together with rates and patterns of GP registration and of hospital use, suggest that access to GP services is better for this group than has been found in other research studies (e.g. Shelter, 2000). All accommodation providers and day centres visited were very proactive in terms of GP registration. Seventy-seven per cent (n=123) of the young people said that they were registered with a GP[36], and of those who were not, 81 per cent (n=30) said that they knew of a doctor or medical centre that they could use. The highest rate of GP registration (85%) was in Brighton and Hove, where there is a dedicated GP surgery for homeless people. At the remaining three research sites, rates of registration varied between 70 per cent and 78 per cent, and GPs were accessed in a variety of locations, including at regular surgeries at day centres and hostels.

Barriers to general health service access

Hinton *et al.* (2001) note that homelessness services have contact with people at key times in their lives, such as when first leaving home, becoming homeless, or embarking on independent living for the first time. These represent opportunities to ensure that they have health information and support when they are most likely to need and use it.

When asked about access to health care some young people acknowledged that the NHS generally is under strain, and that there are thus problems (for example, waiting lists) for everybody, not just the homeless. They did, however, point to other barriers that limit access to health care, such as:

- stigmatisation by NHS staff (including dental staff) because they were homeless, or substance users, leading to judgemental and non-sympathetic treatment (n=13);
- problems registering with a GP because of the lack of an address (n=10);
- appointment systems and long waits for consultations (n=9); and
- shame and embarrassment at their appearance and situation, which meant they were reluctant to use services (n=3).

The service providers identified the transience of homeless young people as a major barrier to accessing and receiving continuous primary health care. Apart from the difficulties presented when treatment involved follow-up appointments or referral to other services, their

---

36. This generally refers to a three-month 'temporary registration'. Full registration is required for GPs to be able to refer patients to other services and specialists, or to prescribe more than one month's medication.

transience meant that some young people had become completely detached and disengaged from ordinary health services. They therefore suggested that it was vital that homeless young people were linked in to a GP as quickly as is possible.

Providers suggested that there is still some considerable reluctance amongst GPs to work with homeless young people, since they are perceived as being difficult and high-maintenance patients. Attention was drawn to the perception that in many cases, surgery receptionists or other 'gatekeepers' made the decision to allow registration and not the GPs personally, and that the basis for such decisions might be questionable. Some pointed to the training implications for GPs in dealing with this client group. Certainly, some limited work which has been done from a GP perspective (Lester *et al.*, 2002) suggests that they feel untrained to deal with the many problems of homeless people, and also points to concerns over time costs and negative attitudes towards homeless people as being significant issues. Taken together with some of the comments made by the young people which indicate a reluctance to use GP services because of stigmatisation, it would appear that there are barriers to access on both sides (see also Croft-White and Rayner, 1999). Providers also commented on negative attitudes towards the homeless amongst ambulance and A and E staff.

Overall, the barriers faced meant that successful service access could be unpredictable, and it was arbitrary whether, or not, the necessary health care and support were obtained.

Improving access to health services
When asked how access to health services could be improved, the young people suggested:

- more outreach work (particularly regular GP attendance at day centres and hostels) (n=16);
- more funding and service expansion (n=15);
- dedicated surgeries and clinics for homeless young people (n=14);
- changing the attitudes of health service staff towards homeless young people (n=13); and
- more walk-in services (n=9).

Similarly, 12 service providers proposed the increased use of dedicated medical services for homeless young people, and of outreach work and other methods of 'taking the services to the young people'. Five providers emphasised the need to work with services to overcome reluctance and stereotyping, and make them more responsive, so that the young people could be integrated into mainstream primary care. As Lester *et al.*'s (2002) review of primary healthcare provision for homeless people concluded, these providers thought that segregation from mainstream health care was unlikely to resolve the health inequalities of homelessness. The question of whether dedicated or integrated medical services best serve the health needs of homeless young people is clearly a matter which continues to exercise professionals in the field.

Mental health

As described in Chapter 4, the homeless young people experience a diverse range of mental health problems. Seventy young people (44%) had at some stage in their lives received treatment for a mental health problem, over half of whom had done so since becoming homeless (n=45). Of those who had received treatment the majority had been treated in the community by GPs (53%), community psychiatrists (29%) and community counsellors (26%), with only 10 per cent reporting having been psychiatric hospital inpatients. The young people had received a number of different types of treatment: 46 per cent had been prescribed anti-depressants, 44 per cent had attended counselling, and 19 per cent had seen psychiatrists. Other treatments received included anti-psychotic medication and other unspecified therapy.

Providers expressed considerable concerns regarding the difficulties surrounding the identification and treatment of young people with mental health problems, particularly those who were dual diagnosis cases. An initial hurdle to diagnosis of problems was said to be the stigma amongst young people regarding mental illness, which may discourage them from seeking help. It was suggested that there were often young people attending homelessness services with undiagnosed conditions, and that these could also go undetected by service staff. The psychiatric nurse interviewed commented on how both caseload and mental health sections among homeless young people in the area had increased recently, which was attributed in great part to homelessness service staff training in mental health issues, and subsequent increased levels of detection.

Young people who suffered dual diagnosis were said to experience particular barriers to service access; it often appeared to providers that no single agency was willing to take responsibility for, or 'ownership' of, them, and they consequently fell through the gap in services.

Alcohol services

All those young people who described their alcohol use as a problem, or who said that they thought they currently or had ever needed help with their drinking, were asked about their use of alcohol services. In total this included 20 young people. One current drinker who felt their drinking warranted anger management rather than alcohol services and one ex-drinker who stated that he had used a service (residential treatment) to stop drinking were not included. Overwhelmingly, those young people who had ceased to use alcohol said that they had 'just stopped', and had sought no help at all.

Table 5.2: **Use of alcohol services[1]**

Service type	% ever used (n=20)	% used in the last month (n=20)	% aware of service could use (n=20)	% would use in future (n=20)
Drop-in, information and counselling	50	20	75	60
AA or self help group	20	5	75	45
Residential alcohol detoxification	15	0	45	45
Community detoxification	15	0	30	35
Residential treatment	10	0	30	45
Day programme	5	0	30	45

Note:
1. Interviewees were able to give multiple responses.

Although levels of service awareness were high amongst the 20 respondents, levels of actual use were much lower, with the exception of drop-in, information and counselling services. There was a general perception that alcohol services were in the main intended for, and used by, older drinkers. Drop-in services were much more likely to be used, and to be described as friendly and 'always there when you need them'. Some young people had accessed help with drinking through other means; two had been referred after consulting their GP, and a further two mentioned advice they had received from a youth service and a college advisor.

Barriers to alcohol services access

There was therefore evidence of some reluctance to use alcohol services. The young people (n=20) identified the following barriers:

- their own lack of motivation (n=5);
- inability to secure funding for residential detox and treatment (n=4);
- a preference to 'do things themselves' (n=3);
- negative perceptions of services and service users (n=2);
- long waiting lists (n=1);
- having to be 'dry' to access residential services (n=1); and
- too many rules and regulations (n=1).

Service providers were also asked about homeless young people's use of alcohol services. They referred to the lack of dedicated services available. Providers thought that services were in general geared towards the treatment of alcoholism, rather than alcohol issues and problems. They were therefore viewed as inappropriate as a response to the drinking behaviour of most homeless young people.

Low levels of service use in part reflect lower levels of need (as perceived or observed by providers) in terms of dependency. However, they also reflected the finding that patterns of drinking, and binge drinking in particular, reported by many young people were not perceived by them as problematic. Homeless young people are not unique in this respect; there is evidence of similar attitudes to binge and heavy drinking amongst young people more generally, amid concerns about the prevalence of such behaviour (Alcohol Concern, 2002).

Improving access to alcohol services

When asked how services and service access might be improved, the young people (n=20) suggested:

- dedicated/discrete services for young people (n=4);
- more drop-in and counselling services (n=3);
- more 'wet'[37] day centres and accommodation (n=1); and
- more service funding and more services (n=1).

The service providers made very similar suggestions, emphasising discrete service provision. Additionally, they highlighted the usefulness of brief interventions work and diversionary

---

37. In 'wet' services service users are permitted to use alcohol on the premises.

activities, and noted that there may be a place for more 'wet' service provision since the police are now increasingly enforcing public drinking bans. Providers saw their roles as providing continuing support for those who did seek help with their drinking, and building the motivation of those who were 'not yet ready' to do so.

Drugs services

A total of 44 young people who had either defined their use of drugs as problematic, or said that they thought that they had ever needed help or treatment, were asked about their use of drugs services. There was only one interviewee defined as a problem user by the research team who did not consider their use of drugs to be a problem and they were also included. One person declined to answer these questions.

Table 5.3:   Use of drugs services[1]

Service type	% ever used (n=44)	% used in the last month (n=44)	% aware of service could use (n=44)	% would use in future (n=44)
Drop-in advice, information and counselling	80	30	80	73
GP	80	27	91	70
Methadone maintenance or reduction	39	7	68	48
Detox	20	0	55	66
Narcotics Anonymous or self-help group	16	5	59	45
Day programme	14	2	52	39
Residential treatment	11	2	55	66

Note:
1. Interviewees were able to give multiple responses.

Other than the services they were specifically asked about, young people also reported receiving help from homelessness agency staff, and from family members. The most positive views were expressed about drop-in and counselling services. Despite reasonable levels of awareness of services, ranging from 52 per cent to 91 per cent dependent on service type, and an expressed willingness to use them in future, recent levels of reported service use were very low.

The only exception to this was in respect of needle exchanges, which had been used by 20 of the 23 IDUs in the past month. Only one IDU was unaware of a needle exchange they could use.

Barriers to drugs service access

The young people identified a number of barriers to accessing the different sources of help (n=44, see Table 5.3).

- long waiting lists for detoxification, community and residential services, and it was often difficult to get funding for these (n=15);
- GPs were felt to be insufficiently informed about drug use, and users' needs and problems; they, and their staff, were viewed as generally unsympathetic and negative in attitude towards drug users (n=13);
- concerns about the health implications of methadone prescribing, and that this just meant 'swapping one addiction for another' (n=11);
- a dislike of the ethos and approaches adopted by some services, for example, 12-step programmes' (n=7);
- a preference to 'do things themselves' (n=7);
- rigid appointment systems and referral procedures were frequently mentioned (n=7);
- a desire to avoid, rather than associate with, other drug users, and hence they were unwilling to access drugs services where they would inevitably come into contact with other users (n=5); and
- previous 'failures' or bad experiences using drugs services (n=2);

Low levels of drugs service access (apart from needle exchange services) by homeless drug users generally have also been reported by other studies (Willis, 1999; Fountain and Howes, 2002). This could reasonably be expected to be an even more acute problem amongst homeless young people, since there is a dearth of services aimed at young substance users specifically, and the evidence is that those that do exist are not well used (Ashton, 1999).

Providers suggested that difficulties relating to detection and disclosure of drug use sometimes precluded any attempts to offer help. It was not always easy to ascertain whether or not a young person was using drugs, and concerns about exclusion from homeless services were thought to act as a deterrent to disclosure. Irrespective of this, the nature and operation of available drugs service provision generated a number of criticisms. Providers saw provision as limited for young people; there were also insufficient residential and detoxification beds available, and a lack of choice of treatment models. The hurdle of delay was frequently mentioned; waiting lists and lengthy referral procedures meant that the need to capitalise on motivation at the moment it was expressed was ignored and opportunities to intervene effectively with the young people were missed. Problems identified in relation to working partnerships with drugs agencies were not related to the actual partnerships themselves, but to the processes involved.

Homelessness service workers' knowledge and awareness of local drugs services was variable, and most available provision was thought to be for 'hard end' opiate users. Respondents also pointed to what they saw as a staffing crisis in the drugs field, both in terms of numbers, and of appropriate training, which was affecting the range, quality and effectiveness of the services available.

Voluntary take-up of drugs services by homeless young people was said to be low, but providers thought that 'most go willingly' if referred, and if they continue to receive encouragement and support. However, providers thought that a major barrier to seeking help was the perception amongst people that their use of drugs was recreational, rather than problematic. Providers suggested that sometimes denial of problem use was a strategy to avoid facing the pain of addressing associated problems.

There was view amongst providers that age was an important factor in terms of how drug use was perceived and experienced. Many young people were not thought to be very knowledgeable about drugs, and perhaps tended to think themselves invincible to dependency problems, and thus it was often hard to 'get the messages across'. Providers thought many would only learn from experience, and it would often take a major life event, such as the death of a friend, for change to occur.

Improving access to drugs services

When asked how drugs service access might be improved, the 44 young people made the following suggestions:

- more 'one-to-one' and drop-in services, with more ex-user drug workers (n=6);
- improved funding and expansion of services so that they would be 'there when you need them' (n=6);
- activities to fill the time otherwise spent using drugs (n=5);
- more outreach work so young people do not have to attend drugs agencies (n=3);

- needle exchanges open more often (n=3);
- dedicated services for young people (n=1); and
- more relapse prevention work (n=1).

The service providers also suggested ways to improve access. The responses to drug use needed to be made in relation to other problems that the young people were facing, and their youth. Furthermore, these responses needed to be both rapid and flexible. Often the response required was not treatment as such, but diversion, education or harm reduction. Each of these was thought to be best facilitated by dedicated services (or at the very least by having dedicated young peoples' workers in drugs agencies), and by bringing the drugs services to the young people at the homelessness agencies. These models are already in operation in some services. More innovative approaches, such as buddying, or mentoring, were proposed, as were attempts at different forms of diversion, for example, football teams and music projects.

6.   Preventing problem substance use and reducing harm

Examining the concept of prevention

Chapter 3 explored young people's differing patterns of substance use. Due to this variation any consideration of prevention work with homeless young people needs to begin by acknowledging their diverse experiences, as well as their shared problems and needs related to their homeless status. There is a growing recognition of the need for messages to be targeted at specific groups, with more emphasis being placed on distinguishing between non-users and different types of users (ACMD, 1998). Prevention activity can be defined as activities that stop, or reduce the frequency of, use of illegal substances[38]. Prevention programmes often address the symptoms of substance use, for example highlighting the possibility of health problems, and attempt to deter young people from becoming involved in substance use, or to steer them towards less risky patterns of substance use. If delivered in tandem with responses that address the needs and problems of homeless young people, the range of factors underlying substance use can be worked upon. In summary, the purpose of prevention can be to prevent use, to reduce use, to encourage safer use and to provide harm/risk minimisation (Welsh Drug and Alcohol Unit, 1999). Prevention activity may include the following:

- Primary: to stop people starting.
- Secondary: to minimise risk and reduce demand.
- Tertiary: to start people stopping and avoid further harm.

Using the above definition there is some commonality between secondary and tertiary prevention and treatment for substance users. Whilst treatment frequently aims to achieve abstinence, it is recognised that this will not be an immediate, appropriate nor effective aim for some individuals. Thus treatment may be geared to the reduction of harm to both the user and others.

---

38.   It can also refer to the misuse of legal substances.

Young people's knowledge about substances

The 160 interviewees were asked to specify up to three sources of their information on substances. The most common responses are summarised below.

- Experience (44%): The finding that many were obtaining information about substances through experimenting fits with the finding that 61 per cent of the sample suggested that they did not have much information about drugs before they started using. This has major implications for young people in terms of their exposure to risk, and it suggests the need for drug education to be delivered at an early age or at the time when they are considering substance use. However, given the widespread use of drugs amongst this group, it is possible that experience may override other sources of information.
- Literature (27%): This includes leaflets and posters and it is likely that young people have accessed some of these through homelessness agencies.
- Friends (22%): This reaffirms the finding of many studies of young people that the peer group is an important source of information. Whilst young people can deliver prevention messages as many peer education projects demonstrate, it is also possible that friendship networks can perpetuate myths about substance use (Shiner, 2000).
- School (10%): This figure is low but many of the sample are likely to have had disrupted educational careers and some attended school prior to the widespread introduction of compulsory drug education in primary and secondary schools in 1995 (DfEE, 1995).

Examining the impact of prevention messages

Chapter 3 explored the drug using behaviour of homeless young people. This analysis suggested that at least some young people had taken on board prevention messages. For example, 20 of the injecting drug users (87%) appeared to recognise the importance of accessing clean needles and disposing of them safely. Here we focus on young people's assessment of the impact of information they had received on their drug use. Just over one-third (35%) of the sample were able to identify receiving specific information which had led to a change in their behaviour in some way. The information identified came from a variety of sources. The most frequently mentioned was acquiring knowledge from friends and acquaintances about the risks of taking particular drugs. Other sources of information included drugs awareness courses, leaflets, posters and magazines, and drugs treatment services. The information received impacted on the young people in a variety of ways; in particular it led to them avoiding certain drugs, using drugs in safer ways, limiting the amount of drugs they took and generally becoming more wary of drugs they used.

Their responses suggest that at least some young people might be willing to engage with prevention activities because they have responded to information given in the past. Five individuals stated that they had given up drug use altogether in response to information received. Expecting young people to give up drugs is perhaps unrealistic but appropriately delivered harm reduction messages may be effective at steering young people away from the most harmful drugs and encourage safer use of substances.

Current prevention and harm reduction activity

Interviews with service providers included questions about current prevention activities with service users. The following activities were identified as prevention activities. Only the first two were done frequently.

1. Provision of information e.g. offering leaflets.
2. Informal discussions through one-to-one work.
3. Formal prevention activities e.g. drugs awareness talks and workshops (including theatre-based ones); peer education with harm reduction messages related to injecting and overdose.

Formal prevention activities were rare, and the view was sometimes expressed that young people do not engage with this approach and resist being lectured to. Successful strategies have been identified as interactive, user-friendly, non-judgemental, accessible, fun, interesting and relevant (Welsh Drug and Alcohol Unit, 1999). This squares with the views of one service provider who noted that the best prevention messages are those that are delivered in subtle and indirect ways, avoiding scare tactics and judgmental attitudes and advocating moderation rather than abstinence.

Harm reduction work can involve a range of simple practical acts, as well as attempts to change the behaviour of young people. These have to be done within the constraints of criminal law. The provision of clean needles is perhaps the best known example of this. Injecting drugs exposes people to a wide range of health risks. These include the transmission of blood-borne viral inflections, namely HIV, hepatitis B and C. Whilst there are no vaccinations for HIV and hepatitis C, one is available for hepatitis B. This is a serious virus, which can cause liver damage and sometimes result in death. It is, however, preventable through immunisation (Derricot *et al.*, 2001). Interviewees were asked if they had been offered any immunisations since they had been homeless. Only 11 respondents had been offered the hepatitis B vaccination and all but one of these had taken up this offer. This constitutes only 24 per cent of those who had ever injected. This suggests missed opportunities for harm reduction work with injecting drug users.

The potential for future prevention activity with homeless young people

There is considerable scope for prevention activity with young homeless people but there are some major obstacles to overcome. Respondents were asked whether they wanted more information about tobacco, alcohol and drugs. Only 27 per cent (n=43) of the sample (30% of those who had used in the last week) stated that they wanted more information about drugs. Lower proportions agreed that they would like more information about alcohol (19% (n=27) of current drinkers) or tobacco (14% (n=24) of current smokers). Those that argued that they did not want more information included those using them safely, for example those drinking alcohol within sensible limits. However, the low levels of requests for more information also suggests that some young homeless people may be resistant to engaging in prevention activities even though they might benefit from them.

The young people who suggested they wanted more information about substances were given the opportunity to specify where they would obtain this from (up to three choices were allowed). The most common responses are summarised below.

- Drugs agency (n=40)
- GP (n=34)
- Hostels and night shelters (n=32)
- Day centre (n=18)

Given that many of the young people interviewed are not in contact with drugs services it is surprising that one-quarter identified a drugs agency as a place they would go to obtain information. In some respects it constitutes the obvious answer to the question, which may in part explain why it was so frequently given. However, it does point to the need for agencies to provide advice and information as part of their package of treatment activities. The number of young people who suggested they would ask their GP is also higher than anticipated because a commonly acknowledged problem is the reluctance of GPs to work with drug users (Lester *et al.*, 2002). It appears that approximately one-fifth of the sample perceived a GP as an approachable expert on the health risks of substance use. This may be because they often visited the doctor's surgery due to ongoing health problems or had the opportunity to have regular contact with a GP through surgeries held in day centres. A slightly larger proportion of young people stated that they would consult a GP in Brighton (32%)[39].

Overall the most frequently mentioned sources of information about substance use were homelessness agencies. This suggests that prevention work can take place within homelessness agencies but at present this is likely to be hampered by the limited knowledge of some agency staff. The interviews revealed that some service providers had little understanding of the concept of prevention. Some equated it solely with discouraging young people from using drugs in the first place, and in part this reflects the lack of training they had received. Only two-thirds of the service providers interviewed had received any training although all had built up knowledge of substance use issues through other means.

- Two identified themselves as ex-problem substance users.
- Many had considerable experience of working with homeless substance users, including four individuals who had worked in substance use agencies.
- Other strategies included establishing informal links with workers in drugs agencies, obtaining relevant literature from specialist agencies and 'keeping an ear to the street'.

In order to respond to the needs of homeless young people using substances, agencies adopted a number of working models. Five agencies had employed specialist drugs workers, but the typical model was to refer young people to local treatment agencies. In some instances the knowledge of workers was restricted to a vague awareness of the work of one or two drugs treatment agencies but staff in other agencies had developed good working relationships. Whilst partnership working is important, to be effective this model requires generic workers to have sufficient training to identify potential substance use problems and to encourage young people to access treatment services, if appropriate.

---

39. This may be explained by the presence of a doctor's surgery specifically for the homeless staffed by professionals who had proven they were willing to work with problem drug users.

7. Summary and recommendations

Key findings

Substance use

Homeless young people reported high lifetime, last year and last month prevalence rates for drugs (illegal drugs and illicit use of prescribed medication). Ninety-five per cent of young people had used drugs. Often they had begun experimenting with illegal drugs at a young age, typically aged 14. Levels of use of cannabis, amphetamine and ecstasy were particularly high, but a substantial minority had used heroin and crack cocaine. Current patterns of drug use were diverse. Seventeen per cent of the sample were identified as problem drug users and a further 14 per cent had been problem drug users in the past. Whilst many drug users took measures to ensure that their drug taking was as safe as possible, the data gathered suggests evidence of some risky behaviours. These include poly-drug use and unsafe injecting practices. Almost one-quarter (23%) had accidentally overdosed on drugs or alcohol.

Almost all the young people interviewed smoked on a daily basis. It was evident that many young people were increasing the health risks of smoking by smoking hand-rolled cigarettes without filters and mixing tobacco with illegal drugs. Current patterns of alcohol use were diverse. Whilst 18 per cent of the sample did not drink at all, a considerable proportion were adopting risky drinking patterns: frequently exceeding sensible daily limits and binge drinking. Fourteen per cent of the sample was identified as problem drinkers.

Homelessness

The young people interviewed frequently became homeless for the first time at an early age, and for over half the sample this followed episodes of running away. Substance use was the second most common explanation for homelessness but this was not always problem substance use, and sometimes was only one of a number of reasons given. Other common reasons for becoming homeless were family conflict and experiences of abuse. Experiences of rough sleeping at some point in their lives amongst the sample were high. This reflects the finding they sometimes became homeless with little warning and were not aware of where they could go to get help. Young people faced multiple barriers when attempting to access temporary and permanent accommodation. Substance use was cited by the young people as one of many barriers they faced, and service providers echoed this view.

Consequences of homelessness and substance use

The relationship between substance use and homelessness is complex, and the young people's accounts suggest that whilst becoming homeless can lead to an escalation of substance use it can also provide an opportunity to give up or cut down.

One-fifth of interviewees who reported health problems attributed them solely to substance use. Homelessness, particularly sleeping rough, appeared to have a detrimental effect on the physical health of almost half the young people interviewed. Poor access to health care was rarely mentioned as a problem. Instead young people felt other aspects of homelessness had a greater impact such as poor diets and lack of shelter and warmth. Levels of mental health problems were disproportionately high amongst young homeless people.

The use of alcohol and drugs had consequent implications for offending. Ninety-five per cent of young people had committed an offence at some point in their lives. A quarter of young people linked these offences with alcohol use and half with drug use. Experiences of victimisation were also common amongst the sample.

Access to services

The strongest message emerging from the research regarding service access was the need for dedicated and appropriate provision for young people, which addresses their substance use within the context of the many other problems that they experience. This applies equally to homelessness and substance misuse services.

Prevention of substance use

Prevention activities with homeless young people were limited but there is considerable scope for prevention work with this group. However, there are a number of barriers to successful prevention work, particularly the possibility of resistance from some young people, legal constraints and the lack of expertise in many homelessness services.

Policy recommendations

In this section, consideration is given to the implications of these key findings for the promotion of good practice under a number of broad headings. There is no attempt to identify those responsible for each of the recommendations. However, the key players in tackling problem substance use and homelessness are substance use services; drug action teams; homelessness agencies; local authorities and other providers of social housing and health services. The importance of partnerships between agencies in order to be able to respond appropriately and adequately to the needs of homeless young people cannot be overemphasised. Partnership should be central to all service planning, design and delivery. It is important that the key players, individually and collectively, develop strategies to tackle homelessness, problem substance use and related issues. For example, the Support and Housing Needs Assessment Project has developed a common assessment form for homelessness agencies in Cardiff to enable them to share information.

In this section the recommendations are set out under neatly defined headings, but like Fountain and Howes (2002) the findings presented in this report suggest that the complexity of the problems experienced by homeless young people need to form the backdrop to any discussion of how best to proceed.

Tackling substance use
Drugs
The findings of this study suggest the need for the following specific types of prevention work with homeless young people:

- early interventions, or interventions at a time when young people are considering drug use;
- highlighting the possible dangers of poly-drug use;
- raising awareness of the health risks of problem drug use, particularly injecting;
- reminding injecting drug users of safer injecting practices and the importance of avoiding injecting in the presence of others because of the risk that it might lead to others injecting. The Break the Cycle campaign promoted by DrugScope and supported by the Department of Health aims to prevent current injectors from injecting in front of non-injectors and help them to resist giving people their first injection through a brief intervention (see Hunt *et al.*, 2001 for further information);
- promoting awareness of ways of avoiding accidental overdoses and providing drug users with the necessary skills to cope with incidents of overdose by their peers. The *Big Issue* in Brighton had offered two training sessions run by NHS drug workers, which aimed to provide accurate and concise information on the risks associated with drug use and to suggest strategies for reducing harm, including preventing overdose. It also included how to deal with overdose (see Hunter and Power, 2002 for further information); and

- providing information on harm reduction, effects of drug use, treatment and advice services in drugs agencies, GP surgeries and homelessness agencies.

There is additional scope for interventions with service providers to enhance their ability to work with substance users and those at risk of becoming substance users, including:

- training all homelessness service providers around substance use issues, and raising their awareness of locally available services in order to facilitate appropriate referrals;
- clear and definitive Home Office guidance regarding the implementation of Section 8 of the Misuse of Drugs Act 1971. Despite the passage of three years since the Wintercomfort case, the research found that providers' concerns around this issue have not diminished.

Alcohol

Given the findings of this study it would appear that prevention activity aimed at this group needs to emphasise the dangers of binge drinking and to encourage drinking within sensible daily limits, and in particular such interventions need to be targeted at young males.

Tobacco

Whilst it would be preferable to support young people in their attempts to give up smoking, for example through the provision of no smoking areas in hostels and day centres, inevitably some young people will continue to smoke. Hence harm reduction activity could be geared towards highlighting the dangers of smoking cigarettes without filters and mixing tobacco with drugs.

Providing treatment for substance use

Providing appropriate treatment services that address substance use and recognise the complexity of other issues experienced by homeless young people could be achieved in a number of ways:

- discrete, dedicated services for young people;
- appointment of dedicated young people's workers in substance use agencies;
- bringing the services to homeless young people at homelessness service premises by means of regular sessions and surgeries run by primary care, drugs and alcohol services' workers and through outreach work at young peoples' centres;

- expanding drop-in services;
- more innovative work with young substance users, for example mentoring or diversion activities such as music or sport which aim to encourage young people to develop interests other than substance use.

Homelessness prevention and services

The ideal situation is to prevent young people becoming homeless in the first place, and action needs to be put in place, targeting in particular those young people at risk of becoming homeless such as 'looked after' young people, runaways and drug users. Early interventions can facilitate young people being able to retain their current accommodation, for example by preventing illegal evictions and helping them to manage rent arrears. The widespread provision of drop-in advice centres for young people (or 'one stop shops') where they can access advice on a range of issues is one possible model. An example of this approach is the Youth Advice Centre (YAC) in Brighton and Hove, managed by the YMCA.

It is inevitable that some young people will become homeless and our findings suggest the need for the following actions:

- developing services such as mediation schemes, drop-in advice and short-term accommodation for young people who become homeless before they are 16;
- prioritising of support for young rough sleepers so that rough sleeping is a short-lived experience;
- providing of dedicated homelessness services for young people aged between 16 and 25; and
- promoting awareness of services that are available for homeless young people so young people do not find themselves in situations where they have no one to turn to.

The data gathered suggested that once young people have accommodation they find it difficult to retain it. Hence floating support packages to enable them to sustain tenancies in social or private housing, and supported housing may be appropriate for some groups of young people.

Housing policy

In the literature on homelessness a political model has emerged that explains homelessness with reference to the manner in which changing structural conditions impact most severely upon particular groups. This is either because of a simple position of structural disadvantages or because some further vulnerability renders a person especially ill equipped to cope with those changes (May, 2000; Pleace *et al.*, 1997). The young people interviewed were vulnerable in many respects although they rarely met the vulnerability criteria determined by local authorities. It was also evident that a number of structural conditions were impacting on this group. Some of these problems are not peculiar to young people, such as the lack of affordable accommodation in the private sector and the shortage of social housing. However, the difficulties they faced in finding housing were exacerbated by current benefit policies, particularly the single room rent, which is in need of review.

Promoting health

Some of the difficulties traditionally experienced by homeless people in terms of accessing health care have been overcome by the provision of dedicated GP surgeries for homeless people or more commonly by GPs and nurses offering clinics in day centres for homeless people. Difficulties remain in accessing mental health services and this needs urgent attention. This might include increasing the knowledge base of staff in homelessness agencies on mental health issues so they can identify young people experiencing mental health problems and dual diagnosis, as well as being alert to issues of suicide and self-harm. The research also suggests the need for education and training amongst general health professionals and their staff, aimed at eliminating the stereotypical and negative attitudes and beliefs about homeless young people which seem so often to represent a barrier to service access. However, promoting health amongst homeless young people is not simply about promoting access to health care. It requires tackling the other health inequalities they experience. This might included providing vitamins to compensate for poor diets, offering vaccinations to reduce exposure to disease and trying to create healthier environments in hostels and night shelters. Health problems are bound up with other aspects of the lives of young people, including substance use, and therefore need to be addressed in this context.

Service type	Description
Night shelters	Provide overnight accommodation, usually on a first-come, first served basis.
Emergency bed unit[40]	Emergency facility providing temporary accommodation.
Day centres	Provide advice, support, food, washing and laundry facilities, activities; host sessions run by other agencies (e.g. health, substance use).
Hostels	Provide temporary accommodation and support; host sessions run by other agencies.
Supported housing	Provide temporary accommodation; on-site or floating support of varies intensities.
Foyer	Provide temporary accommodation linked in with education, employment and training.
Outreach teams	Work on the streets and in partnership with other agencies to make contact with homeless people and facilitate service access.
Drop-in	Centres providing advice, advocacy, support and referrals.
Big Issue	Provide the opportunity for homeless people to make an income. Campaign on behalf of homeless people. Services also provide advice, support and referrals.

40.   Unique to one research site.

Appendix B

The young people interviewed were asked about the use of each of the drugs included in the British Crime Survey (BCS) in their lifetime, the last year and last month so that the data could be compared with BCS data for young people aged between 16 and 25. In order to gain more detailed information about their current drug use respondents were also asked about their drug use in the last week.

Several minor modifications were made to the BCS questions after the pilot to include the use of painkillers such as DF118 (dihydrocodeine tartrate), and tranquillisers that were not prescribed. Less frequently used drugs such as PCP (phencyclidine), ketamine, and GHB (gammahydroxybutyrate) were also included because they were mentioned in some of the early interviews and the latter two are thought to be becoming more prevalent albeit on a small scale (DrugScope, 2001). A decision was also taken to exclude 'semeron', a dummy drug used in the comparable BCS data to identify those exaggerating their drug use. The young people were instead asked which drugs they did not recognise[41].

The data collected for this study also differed from the BCS 2000 data in a number of other important respects. Self-reported data can be used as a reliable indicator of drug use by adolescents (Oetting and Beauvais, 1990). However, respondents to the BCS were asked these questions in the context of a victimisation survey, which is likely to lead to under-reporting of drug use (Ramsay et al., 2001). In contrast the young people were aware that this study focused solely on their substance use, and their decision to be interviewed may have reflected their willingness to disclose this behaviour. Laptop computers were used to enable respondents to self-complete the drug use component of the BCS. We asked the young people these questions face-to-face in order to ensure that they were understood. Subsequently, the young people were asked very detailed questions regarding their substance use so it is likely to have become apparent to the interviewer if they were not truthful in their responses. Finally in the BCS the prevalence rates in the last year were based on the last calendar year rather than the 12 months prior to the interview used in this study because it is easier to recollect (Kershaw et al., 2001)[42]. For a more detailed discussion of the validity of self-reported data, particularly the BCS, see Aldridge et al., 1999.

---

41. Since 2001 this method has also been used in the BCS.
42. Since 2001 this method has also been used in the BCS.

References

Advisory Council on the Misuse of Drugs (1998) *Drug Misuse and the Environment*. London: HMSO.

Alcohol Concern (2002) *The State of the Nation: Britain's True Alcohol Bill*. London: Alcohol Concern.

Aldridge, J., Parker, H. and Measham, F. (1999) *Drug Trying and Drug Use Across Adolescence*. London: Drug Prevention Advisory Service.

Ashton, M (1999) 'Between two stools: children, drugs policy and professional practice' in A. Marlow and G. Pearson (eds.) *Young People, Drugs and Community Safety*. Lyme Regis: Russell House Publishing.

Big Issue in the North (1999) *Drugs at the Sharp End*. Manchester: *Big Issue* in the North.

Bines, W. (1994) *The Health of Single Homeless People*. York: Centre for Housing Policy.

Brown, S., Cleghorn, A., Schukit, M., Myers, M. and Mott, M. (1996) 'Conduct disorder among adolescent alcohol and drug misusers', *Journal of Studies on Alcohol* 57: 314-424.

Buckland, G. (2002) *Out of the Frying Pan into the Fire? Victimisation and the Young Homeless*, Poster presented at the 2002 British Society of Criminology Conference, Keele University, unpublished.

Buckland, G., Wincup, E. and Bayliss, R. (2002) 'Excluding the excluded: working with homeless drug users', *Criminal Justice Matters*, 47:12-13.

Carlen, P. (1996) *Jigsaw: A Political Criminology of Youth Homelessness*. Buckingham: Open University Press.

Clayton, R. (1992) 'Transitions in drug use: risk and protective factors', in Glantz, M. and Pickens, R. (eds.) *Vulnerability to Drug Abuse*. Washington, D.C.: American Psychology Association.

Cornwell, J. (1984) *Hard-Earned Lives: Accounts of Health and Illness from East London.* London: Tavistock.

Cox, G. and Lawless, M. (1999) *Wherever I Lay my Hat . . . . A Study of Out of Home Drug Users.* Dublin: The Merchant's Quay Project.

Craig, T., Hodson, S., Woodward, S. and Richardson, S. (1996) *Off to a Bad Start: A Longitudinal Study of Homeless Young People in London.* London: Mental Health Foundation.

Craig, T. and Hodson, S. (1998) 'Homeless youth in London: 1. childhood antecedents and psychiatric disorder', *Psychological Medicine,* 28: 1379-1388.

Croft-White, C. and Rayner, G. (1999) *London Health Strategy: Rapid Review of Health and Homelessness.* London: NHS Executive.

Deehan, A. (1999) *Alcohol and Crime: Taking Stock.* London: Home Office.

Department for Education and Employment (1995) *Circular 4/95, Drug Prevention and Schools.* London: HMSO.

Department of Health (1998) *Smoking Kills: A White Paper on Tobacco.* London: The Stationery Office.

Department of Health (1999) *Saving Lives: Our Healthier Nation.* London: Department of Health.

Department of Health (2002) *Smoking, Drinking and Drug Use among Young People in England 2001.* London: Department of Health.

Derricot *et al.* (2001) *Promoting Hepatitis B Immunisation.* London: Exchange Campaigns.

DrugScope (2000) *Homelessness and Drugs: Managing Incidents.* London: Drugscope.

DrugScope (2001) *Annual Report on the Drug Situation 2001.* London: DrugScope.

European Monitoring Centre for Drugs and Drug Addiction (1999) *Extended Annual Report on the State of the Drugs Problem in the European Union 1999.* Luxembourg: Office for Official Publications of the European Communities.

Evans, N. and Dowler, E. (1999) 'Food, health and eating among single homeless and marginalised people in London', *Journal of Human Nutrition and Dietetics,* 12: 179-1999.

Fitzpatrick, S. and Klinker, C. (2000) *Research on Single Homelessness in Britain.* London: Joseph Rowntree Foundation.

Flemen, K. (1997) *Smoke and Whispers: Drugs and Youth Homelessness in Central London.* London: Turning Point.

Flemen, K. (1999) *Room for Drugs. Drug Use on the Premises: Guidelines for Direct Access Services.* London: Release.

Flood-Page, C., Campbell, S., Harrington, V. and Miller, J. (2000) *Youth Crime: Findings from the 1998/99 Youth Lifestyles Survey.* London: Home Office.

Fountain, J. and Howes, S. (2002) *Home and Dry? Homelessness and Substance Use.* London: Crisis.

Goddard, E. and Thomas, M. (1999) *Drinking: Adults' Behaviour and Knowledge in 1998.* London: The Stationery Office.

Goddard, E. and Higgins, V. (2001) *Smoking, Drinking and Drug Use amongst Young People in England in 2000.* London: The Stationery Office.

Goulden, C. and Sondhi, A. (2001) *At the Margins: Drug Use by Vulnerable Groups in the 1998/99 Youth Lifestyles Survey.* London: Home Office.

Graham, J. and Bowling, B. (1995) *Young People and Crime.* London: Home Office.

Grenier, P. (1996) *Still Dying for a Home.* London: Crisis.

Hammersley, R. and Pearl, S. (1997) 'Show me the way to go home: young homeless and drugs', *Druglink,* 12: 11-13.

Health Advisory Service (2001) *The Substance of Young Needs.* London: Health Advisory Service.

Hinton, T., Evans, N. and Jacobs, K. (2001) *Healthy Hostels: A Guide to Promoting Health and Well-being Among Homeless People.* London: Crisis.

Homelessness Directorate. (2002) *More than a Roof: A Report into Tackling Homelessness.* London: ODPM.

Hunt, N., Derricot, J., Preston, A. and Stillwell, G. (2001) *Break the Cycle: Preventing Initiation into Injecting.* London: Exchange Campaigns.

Hunter, G. and Power, R. (2002) 'Including *Big Issue* vendors in a peer education initiative to reduce drug-related harm: a feasibility study', *Drugs: Education, Prevention and Policy,* 9(1): 57-69.

Hutson, S. and Liddiard, M. (1994) *Youth Homelessness: The Construction of a Social Issue.* London: Macmillan.

Jarvis, M. and Bates, C. (1999) *Why Low Tar Cigarettes Don't Work: How the Tobacco Industry has Fooled the Public?.* London: Action on Smoking and Health.

Kershaw, C., Chivite-Matthews, N., Thomas, C. and Aust, R. (2001) *The 2001 British Crime Survey: First Results, England and Wales.* London: Home Office.

Klee, H. and Morris, J. (1995) 'Factors that characterise street injectors', *Addiction,* 90: 837-841.

Klee, H. and Reid, P. (1998) 'Drugs and youth homelessness: reducing the risk', *Drugs: Education, Prevention and Policy,* 5: 269-280.

Lawrenson, F. (1997) 'Runaway children: whose problem?', *British Medical Journal,* 314: 1004.

Lester, H., Wright, W., and Heath, I. (2002) 'Developments in the provision of primary care for homeless people', *British Journal of General Practice Online,* February 2002.

Lloyd, C. (1998) 'Risk factors for problem drug use: identifying vulnerable groups' *Drugs: Education, Prevention and Policy,* 5: 217-232

May, J. (2000) 'Housing histories and homeless careers: a biographical approach', *Housing Studies,* 15: 613-638.

Measham, F., Parker, H., and Aldridge, J. (1998) *Starting, Switching, Slowing and Stopping.* London: Home Office.

National Assembly for Wales (2000a) *Tackling Substance Misuse in Wales: A Partnership Approach.* Cardiff: National Assembly for Wales.

National Assembly for Wales (2000b) *Rough Sleeping in Wales.* Cardiff: National Assembly for Wales.

National Assembly for Wales (2001) *Homelessness Commission: Final Report.* Cardiff: National Assembly for Wales.

National Assembly for Wales (2002) *Draft National Homelessness Strategy.* Cardiff: National Assembly for Wales.

Neale, J. (2001) 'Homelessness amongst drug users: a double jeopardy explored', *International Journal of Drug Policy,* 12: 253-369.

Newburn, T. and Shiner, M. (2001) *Teenage Kicks? Young People and Alcohol: A Review of the Literature.* York: Joseph Rowntree Foundation.

Oetting, G. and Beauvais, F. (1990) 'Adolescent drug use: findings of national and local surveys', *Journal of Consulting and Clinical Psychology,* 5: 385-394.

Office of National Statistics (2001) *Living in Britain: Results from the 2000/01 General Household Survey.* London: The Stationery Office.

Parker, H., Aldridge, J. and Measham, F. (1998) *Illegal Leisure: The Normalisation of Adolescent Recreational Drug Use.* London: Routledge.

Pleace, N., Burrows, R. and Quilgars, D. (1997) 'Homelessness in contemporary Britain: conceptualisation and measurement', in Burrows, R., Pleace, N. and Quilgars, D. (eds.) *Homelessness and Social Policy.* London: Routledge.

President of the Council (1998) *Tackling Drugs to Build a Better Britain: The Government's Ten-Year Strategy for Tackling Drug Misuse.* London: The Stationery Office.

Ramsay, M., Baker, P., Goulden, C., Sharp, C. and Sondhi, A. (2001) *Drug Misuse declared in 2000: Results from the British Crime Survey.* London: Home Office.

Randall, G. (1998) *Rough Sleeping: A Review of Research.* London: DETR.

Ravenhill, M. (2000) *Routes into Homelessness.* London: CASE and Camden Housing Department.

Research, Development and Statistics Directorate (2000) *Statistics on Race and the Criminal Justice System.* London: Home Office.

Rough Sleepers Unit (1999) *Rough Sleeping: The Government's Strategy.* London: DETR.

Rough Sleepers Unit (2000) *Coming in from the Cold: Progress Report on the Government's Strategy on Rough Sleeping.* London: DETR.

Rough Sleepers Unit (2001) *Coming in from the Cold: Second Progress Report on the Government's Strategy on Rough Sleeping.* London: DETR.

Rugg, J. (2000) *Making Connections: Tackling Youth Homelessness through a Multi-agency Approach.* London: Shelter.

Shelter (2000) *Health and Housing.* London: Shelter.

Shiner, M. (2000) *Doing it for Themselves: An Evaluation of Peer Approaches to Drug Prevention.* London: DPAS.

Welsh Drug and Alcohol Unit (1999) *Steps: Your Guide to Drug and Alcohol Prevention Projects.* Cardiff: WDAU.

Willis, S. (1999) *Meeting the Needs of Homeless People with Problematic Drug or Alcohol Use.* Norwich: UEA Social Work Monograph.

Wincup, E. and Bayliss, R. (2001) 'Problematic substance use and the young homeless: implications for well-being', *Youth and Policy,* 71:44-58.

Wright, L. (1999) *Young People and Alcohol: What 11 to 24-year-olds know, think and do.* London: Health Education Authority.

Notes

RDS Publications

Requests for Publications

Copies of our publications and a list of those currently available may be obtained from:

Home Office
Research, Development and Statistics Directorate
Communication Development Unit
Room 275, Home Office
50 Queen Anne's Gate
London SW1H 9AT
Telephone: 020 7273 2084 (answerphone outside of office hours)
Facsimile: 020 7222 0211
E-mail: publications.rds@homeoffice.gsi.gov.uk

alternatively

why not visit the RDS web-site at
         Internet: http://www.homeoffice.gov.uk/rds/index.htm

where many of our publications are available to be read on screen or downloaded for printing.